T0277800

THE
ILLUSTRATED
ANALECTS

THE
ILLUSTRATED
ANALECTS
SELECTED TEACHINGS

ILLUSTRATED BY NI ZONGFENG
TRANSLATED BY ARTHUR WALEY

Books Beyond Boundaries

ROYAL COLLINS

The Illustrated Analects: Selected Teachings

Illustrated by Ni Zongfeng
Translated by Arthur Waley

First published in 2024 by Royal Collins Publishing Group Inc.
Groupe Publication Royal Collins Inc.
550-555 boul. René-Lévesque O Montréal (Québec)
H2Z1B1 Canada

ISBN: 978-1-4878-1275-1

To find out more about our publications,
please visit www.royalcollins.com.

CONTENTS

Foreword   vii

Book I   <ruby>学<rt>xué</rt></ruby><ruby>而<rt>ér</rt></ruby> (Studying)   1

Book II   <ruby>为<rt>wéi</rt></ruby><ruby>政<rt>zhèng</rt></ruby> (Practice of Government)   15

Book III   <ruby>八<rt>bā</rt></ruby><ruby>佾<rt>yì</rt></ruby> (Eight Rows of Dancers)   29

Book IV   <ruby>里<rt>lǐ</rt></ruby><ruby>仁<rt>rén</rt></ruby> (Benevolent Unity)   35

Book V   <ruby>公<rt>gōng</rt></ruby><ruby>冶<rt>yě</rt></ruby><ruby>长<rt>cháng</rt></ruby> (Gongye Chang, Son-in-Law)   49

Book VI   <ruby>雍<rt>yōng</rt></ruby><ruby>也<rt>yě</rt></ruby> (Ran Yong, Student of Confucius)   55

Book VII   <ruby>述<rt>shù</rt></ruby><ruby>而<rt>ér</rt></ruby> (Transmission)   67

Book VIII   <ruby>泰<rt>tài</rt></ruby><ruby>伯<rt>bó</rt></ruby> (Wu Taibo, Founder of the State of Chu)   79

Book IX   <ruby>子<rt>zǐ</rt></ruby><ruby>罕<rt>hǎn</rt></ruby> (The Master Shunned)   85

Book X   ^{xiāng dǎng} 乡党 (The Xiang and Dang Clans)   93

Book XI   ^{xiān jìn} 先进 (Former Generations)   97

Book XII   ^{yán yuān} 颜渊 (Yan Yuan, Disciple of Confucius)   101

Book XIII   ^{zǐ lù} 子路 (Zi Lu, Student of Confucius)   117

Book XIV   ^{xiàn wèn} 宪问 (Yuan Xian, Student of Confucius)   127

Book XV   ^{wèi líng gōng} 卫灵公 (Duke Ling of Wei)   141

Book XVI   ^{jì shì} 季氏 (Chief of Ji Clan)   153

Book XVII   ^{yáng huò} 阳货 (Yang Huo, Offical in the Ji Clan)   161

Book XVIII   ^{wēi zǐ} 微子 (Wei Zi, Founder of the State of Song)   167

Book XIX   ^{zǐ zhāng} 子张 (Zi Zhang, Student of Confucius)   171

Book XX   ^{yáo yuē} 尧曰 (Yao Spoke)   181

Postscript   190

The Illustrated Analects: Selected Teachings

FOREWORD

Ancient people said, "Half of *The Analects* govern the world" and "Without Confucius, eternity is as long as the night." It's important to know that these are not mere dreams or drunken talk from the ancients. For over two thousand years, Confucius's thoughts have influenced generation after generation, illuminating people's lives. *The Analects* records the words and deeds of Confucius and his disciples, reflecting his philosophical ideas and becoming a classic with immense influence in China.

Mr. Qian Mu once said, "Today's Chinese intellectuals have two major responsibilities: to read *The Analects* themselves and encourage others to read it." It has deeply influenced future generations for over two thousand years since its publication. Mr. Liang Qichao once exclaimed, "Embracing one or two phrases can bring a lifetime of benefits." Therefore, exploring better ways to study and promote *The Analects* is crucial.

Contemporary readers often need the help of annotations by later scholars when reading *The Analects*. While there are numerous translations, illustrated books aiding understanding are rare, especially those that vividly express the meaning of it. There are two main reasons for this: firstly, many expressions of *The Analects* often carry universal philosophical values that are challenging to summarize with concrete images; secondly, there are numerous challenges in the transformation between artistic expression and philosophical expression, such as summarizing visual elements, determining artistic styles, and the interaction between art and thought.

Fortunately, Mr. Ni Zongfeng actively explored and delved deep into contemplation and painstakingly produced *The Illustrated Analects: Selected Teachings*. This is a very rare attempt. He spent eight years on this work, and upon careful reading, we can discern three prominent characteristics from it.

Firstly, the understanding of the original meaning is relatively accurate.

Secondly, the refinement of the visuals is quite typical. The transition from text to images is an artistic leap, representing the author's artistic creation process and the creative transformation of thoughts. Objectively speaking, this is highly commendable and requires significant artistic courage and a high level of artistic attainment. The refinement of visuals must be typical, comprehensive, and based on a profound understanding of the text's original meaning to achieve an expressive effect. For example, in the phrase "可欺也, 不可罔也" ([A gentleman] may be deceived, but cannot be led astray), the author's creative interpretation depicts two people fighting in a clay pot, but in reality, they were "crickets." Such ingenious strokes are not uncommon in this book.

Thirdly, the artistic level of the book is high. The artistic style of the book can be described as "ink-wash comics"—it incorporates the techniques, charm, and aesthetics of Chinese ink-wash painting, as well as the depth, sharpness, and humor of comic works. Among the 158 works, the author employs exaggeration, humor, metaphor, contrast, and other widely appreciated comic language to express the profound and witty ancient classical verses.

This exploration holds extraordinary significance in popularizing classics. Modern artists have been using Chinese ink-wash painting to express cultural and philosophical ideas, with Feng Zikai being a representative. However, Mr. Ni, unlike artists such as Feng Zikai, has a crucial difference: Feng Zikai can be considered as lightly "illustrating," while Ni delves deep into "satire." This style suits classics with solid philosophical content, such as *The Analects*. For instance, in the phrase "学而不思则罔" (He who learns but does not think is lost), the author sharply depicts a bookish character who, while reading, imitates a hen hatching eggs, combining impressionism with realism. The strokes are precise and concise, and the characters' expressions are vivid while adhering closely to the theme and meaning, making it a masterpiece of both thought and art!

Of course, *The Analects* is an essential classic in Chinese traditional culture, with high visibility and readership, subject to varying opinions. Furthermore, using images to express ideas is an exploration, sometimes unavoidably leading to one-sidedness or forced interpretation. These aspects need to be personally experienced and pondered by the readers.

As for myself, I am a complete "outsider" when it comes to arts such as painting and calligraphy. However, with the guidance and recommendations of friends, I deeply admire Mr. Ni's explorations, innovations, and insightful thoughts.

With joy as the prelude, I am expressing my respect!

Professor Yang Chaoming

Vice Chairman of the International Confucian Association,

Vice President of the Chinese Confucius Society

December 29, 2021

Book I

xué ér
学而 (Studying)

读书是为了学更多是为了习学习是为了更好地生活

颂经讲学而篇子曰"学而时习之,不亦说乎"句

有感漫笔壬寅年夏 沙孟海峰

xué ér shí xí zhī
学而时习之

zǐ yuē　　　xué ér shí xí zhī　　bù yì yuè hū
子曰："学而时习之, 不亦说乎？"

The Master said, "To learn and at due times to repeat what one has learnt, is that not after all a pleasure?"

<pre>
yǒu péng zì yuǎn fāng lái
</pre>
有 朋 自 远 方 来

<pre>
zǐ yuē   yǒu péng zì yuǎn fāng lái   bù yì lè hū
</pre>
子曰："有朋自远方来，不亦乐乎？"

The Master said, "That friends should come to one from afar, is this not after all delightful?"

3

我不必明批德行世
奈何他人皆不知
读游恬学而篇
惜真人不知而不愠
辛丑春 江上宗峰

rén bù zhī ér bù yùn
人不知而不愠

zǐ yuē　　rén bù zhī　ér bù yùn　bù yì jūn zǐ hū
子曰：“人不知，而不愠，不亦君子乎？”

The Master said, "To remain unsoured even though one's merits are
unrecognized by others, is that not after all what is expected of a
gentleman?"

xiào tì wéi běn

孝悌为本

yǒu zǐ yuē   xiào tì yě zhě   qí wéi rén zhī běn yú

有子曰："孝弟也者，其为仁之本与！"

Master Yu said, "And surely proper behavior towards parents and elder brothers is the trunk of Goodness?"

摧圆嘈邑变
慶方的人
能使人在
安逸中揭
朱財物与名誉
渍污濯觉心向扁
巧言令色鲜矣仁之句悟画
弘章峰

qiǎo yán lìng sè
巧言令色

zǐ yuē   qiǎo yán lìng sè   xiǎn yǐ rén
子曰："巧言令色，鲜矣仁！"

The Master said, "'Clever talk and a pretentious manner' are seldom
found in the Good."

<ruby>吾<rt>wú</rt></ruby> <ruby>日<rt>rì</rt></ruby> <ruby>三<rt>sān</rt></ruby> <ruby>省<rt>xǐng</rt></ruby> <ruby>吾<rt>wú</rt></ruby> <ruby>身<rt>shēn</rt></ruby>

吾日三省吾身

<ruby>曾<rt>zēng</rt></ruby> <ruby>子<rt>zǐ</rt></ruby> <ruby>曰<rt>yuē</rt></ruby>：" <ruby>吾<rt>wú</rt></ruby> <ruby>日<rt>rì</rt></ruby> <ruby>三<rt>sān</rt></ruby> <ruby>省<rt>xǐng</rt></ruby> <ruby>吾<rt>wú</rt></ruby> <ruby>身<rt>shēn</rt></ruby>——<ruby>为<rt>wèi</rt></ruby> <ruby>人<rt>rén</rt></ruby> <ruby>谋<rt>móu</rt></ruby> <ruby>而<rt>ér</rt></ruby> <ruby>不<rt>bù</rt></ruby> <ruby>忠<rt>zhōng</rt></ruby> <ruby>乎<rt>hū</rt></ruby>？ <ruby>与<rt>yǔ</rt></ruby> <ruby>朋<rt>péng</rt></ruby> <ruby>友<rt>yǒu</rt></ruby> <ruby>交<rt>jiāo</rt></ruby> <ruby>而<rt>ér</rt></ruby> <ruby>不<rt>bù</rt></ruby> <ruby>信<rt>xìn</rt></ruby> <ruby>乎<rt>hū</rt></ruby>？ <ruby>传<rt>chuán</rt></ruby> <ruby>不<rt>bù</rt></ruby> <ruby>习<rt>xí</rt></ruby> <ruby>乎<rt>hū</rt></ruby>？"

Master Tsêng said, "Every day I examine myself on these three points: in acting on behalf of others, have I always been loyal to their interests? In intercourse with my friends, have I always been true to my word? Have I failed to repeat* the precepts that I have been handed down to me?"

---

* And so keep in memory.

7

jié yòng ài rén
节用爱人

zǐ yuē　　　dào qiān shèng zhī guó　　jìng shì ér xìn　　jié yòng ér ài rén　　shǐ mín yǐ shí
子曰："道千乘之国，敬事而信，节用而爱人，使民以时。"

The Master said, "A country of a thousand war-chariots cannot be administered unless the ruler attends strictly to business, punctually observes his promises, is economical in expenditure, shows affection towards his subjects in general, and uses the labour of the peasantry only at the proper times of year."*

---

* Not when they ought to be working in the fields. Bad rulers, on the contrary, listen to music or go hunting when they ought to attending to business, continually employ labour on ostentatious building-schemes, etc.

xíng yǒu yú lì　zé yǐ xué wén
行有余力，则以学文

zǐ yuē　　　dì zǐ　　rù zé xiào　chū zé tì　　jǐn ér xìn　　fàn ài zhòng　ér qīn
子曰："弟子，入则孝，出则悌，谨而信，泛爱众，而亲
rén　xíng yǒu yú lì　zé yǐ xué wén
仁。行有余力，则以学文。"

The Master said, "A young man's duty is to behave well to his parents
at home and to his elders abroad, to be cautious in giving promises
and punctual in keeping them, to have kindly feelings towards
everyone, but seek the intimacy of the Good. If, when all that is
done, he has any energy to spare, then let his study the polite art."*

---

* Lean to recite the *Songs*, practise archery, deportment, and the like.

誠信是一个人无
形的力量

读诗论学而偏于夏
日而言而有信之句有
感涂笔辛丑仲春峰

言而有信
yán ér yǒu xìn

zǐ xià yuē   xián xián yì sè   shì fù mǔ   néng jié qí lì   shì jūn   néng zhì qí
子夏曰："贤贤易色；事父母，能竭其力；事君，能致其
shēn   yǔ péng yǒu jiāo   yán ér yǒu xìn
身；与朋友交，言而有信。"

Tzu-hsia said, "A man who treats his betters as betters, wears an air

of respect, who into serving father and mother, knows how to put

his whole strength, who in the service of his prince will lay down his

life, who in intercourse with friends is true to his word."

<ruby>过<rt>guò</rt></ruby>，<ruby>则<rt>zé</rt></ruby><ruby>勿<rt>wù</rt></ruby><ruby>惮<rt>dàn</rt></ruby><ruby>改<rt>gǎi</rt></ruby>

<ruby>子<rt>zǐ</rt></ruby><ruby>曰<rt>yuē</rt></ruby>："<ruby>君<rt>jūn</rt></ruby><ruby>子<rt>zǐ</rt></ruby><ruby>不<rt>bù</rt></ruby><ruby>重<rt>zhòng</rt></ruby>，<ruby>则<rt>zé</rt></ruby><ruby>不<rt>bù</rt></ruby><ruby>威<rt>wēi</rt></ruby>；<ruby>学<rt>xué</rt></ruby><ruby>则<rt>zé</rt></ruby><ruby>不<rt>bù</rt></ruby><ruby>固<rt>gù</rt></ruby>。<ruby>主<rt>zhǔ</rt></ruby><ruby>忠<rt>zhōng</rt></ruby><ruby>信<rt>xìn</rt></ruby>。<ruby>无<rt>wú</rt></ruby><ruby>友<rt>yǒu</rt></ruby><ruby>不<rt>bù</rt></ruby><ruby>如<rt>rú</rt></ruby><ruby>己<rt>jǐ</rt></ruby><ruby>者<rt>zhě</rt></ruby>。<ruby>过<rt>guò</rt></ruby>，<ruby>则<rt>zé</rt></ruby><ruby>勿<rt>wù</rt></ruby><ruby>惮<rt>dàn</rt></ruby><ruby>改<rt>gǎi</rt></ruby>。"

The Master said, "If a gentleman is frivolous,* he will lose the respect of his inferiors and lack firm ground upon which to build up his education. First and foremost, he must learn to be faithful to his superiors, to keep promises, and to refuse the friendship of all who are not like him.** And if he finds he has made a mistake, then he must not be afraid of admitting the fact and amending his ways."

---

* Irresponsible and unreliable in his dealings with others.
** Of those who still reckon in terms of "profit and loss," and have not take Goodness as their standard.

人与人之间都能做到知礼而行
人们的生活才会和谐美好
漢詒漫筆而需有了曰
有武而漫今事 辛丑年春月
礼之用 和为贵之句
冯善峰

lǐ zhī yòng　　hé wéi guì

礼之用，和为贵

yǒu zǐ yuē　　　lǐ zhī yòng　　hé wéi guì

有子曰："礼之用，和为贵。"

Master Yu said, "In the usages of ritual, it is harmony* that is prized."

---

* Harmony between man and nature; playing the musical mode that harmonizes with the season, wearing seasonable clothes, eating seasonable food, and the like.

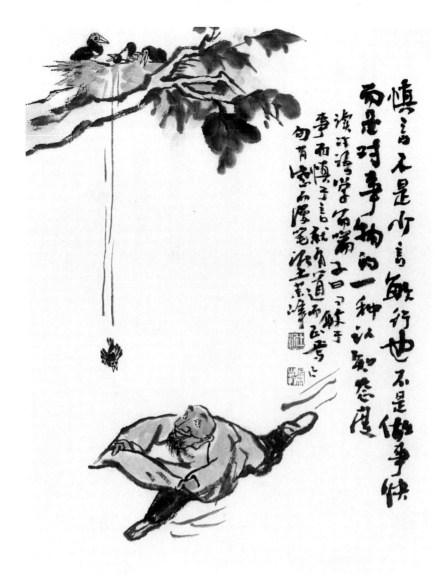

shèn yán mǐn xíng
慎言敏行

zǐ yuē　　　jūn zǐ shí wú qiú bǎo　　jū wú qiú ān　　mǐn yú shì ér shèn yú yán　　jiù yǒu
子曰："君子食无求饱，居无求安，敏于事而慎于言，就有
dào ér zhèng yān　　kě wèi hào xué yě yǐ
道而正焉，可谓好学也已。"

The Master said, "A gentleman who never goes on eating till he is sated, who does not demand comfort in his home, who is diligent in business and cautious in speech, who associates with those that possess the Way and thereby corrects his own faults—such a one may indeed be said to have a taste for learning."

13

huàn bù zhī rén yě
患不知人也

zǐ yuē　　　bù huàn rén zhī bù jǐ zhī　　huàn bù zhī rén yě
子曰："不患人之不己知，患不知人也。"

The Master said, "(the good man) does not grieve that other people do not recognize his merits. His only anxiety is lest he should fail to recognize theirs."

Book II

为政

(Practice of Government)

向着太阳开
百姓跟着恩人走
读论语 为政篇
子曰『为政以德』
句有感漫笔之
辛卯春日月
望景泽

wéi zhèng yǐ dé
为政以德

zǐ yuē wéi zhèng yǐ dé pì rú běi chén jū qí suǒ ér zhòng xīng gòng zhī
子曰："为政以德,譬如北辰,居其所而众星共之。"

The Master said, "He who rules by moral force is like the pole-star, which remains in its place while all the lesser stars do homage to it."

dào zhī yǐ dé, qí zhī yǐ lǐ
道之以德，齐之以礼

子曰："道之以政，齐之以刑，民免而无耻；道之以德，齐之以礼，有耻且格。"

The Master said, "Govern the people by regulations, keep order among them by chastisements, and they will flee from you, and lose all self-respect. Govern them by moral force, keep order among them by ritual and they will keep their self-respect and come to you of their own accord."

shàn huó lè huó
善活乐活

zǐ yuē   wú shí yòu wǔ ér zhì yú xué   sān shí ér lì   sì shí ér bù huò   wǔ shí
子曰："吾十有五而志于学，三十而立，四十而不惑，五十
ér zhī tiān mìng   liù shí ér ěr shùn   qī shí ér cóng xīn suǒ yù   bù yú jǔ
而知天命，六十而耳顺，七十而从心所欲，不逾矩。"

The Master said, "At fifteen, I set my heart upon learning. At thirty, I had planted my feet firm upon the ground. At forty, I no longer suffered from perplexities. At fifty, I knew what were the biddings of Heaven. At sixty, I heard them with docile ear. At seventy, I could follow the dictates of my own heart; for what I desired no longer overstepped the boundaries of right."

<ruby>温<rt>wēn</rt></ruby> <ruby>故<rt>gù</rt></ruby> <ruby>而<rt>ér</rt></ruby> <ruby>知<rt>zhī</rt></ruby> <ruby>新<rt>xīn</rt></ruby>

<ruby>子<rt>zǐ</rt></ruby><ruby>曰<rt>yuē</rt></ruby>: "<ruby>温<rt>wēn</rt></ruby><ruby>故<rt>gù</rt></ruby><ruby>而<rt>ér</rt></ruby><ruby>知<rt>zhī</rt></ruby><ruby>新<rt>xīn</rt></ruby>, <ruby>可<rt>kě</rt></ruby><ruby>以<rt>yǐ</rt></ruby><ruby>为<rt>wéi</rt></ruby><ruby>师<rt>shī</rt></ruby><ruby>矣<rt>yǐ</rt></ruby>。"

The Master said, "He who by reanimating the Old can gain knowledge of the New is fit to be a teacher."

19

jūn zǐ bù qì
君子不器

zǐ yuē   jūn zǐ bù qì
子曰：　"君子不器。"

The Master said, "A gentleman is not an implement."*

---

* A specialist, a tool used for a special purpose. He need only have general, moral qualifications.

20

The Illustrated Analects: Selected Teachings

xiān xíng qí yán　　ér hòu cóng zhī

先行其言，而后从之

zǐ gòng wèn jūn zǐ　　zǐ yuē　　xiān xíng qí yán　　ér hòu cóng zhī

子贡问君子。子曰："先行其言，而后从之。"

Tzu-kung asked about the true gentleman. The Master said, "He does not preach what he practises till he has practised what he preaches."

jūn zǐ zhōu ér bù bǐ
君子周而不比

zǐ yuē   jūn zǐ zhōu ér bù bǐ   xiǎo rén bǐ ér bù zhōu
子曰："君子周而不比，小人比而不周。"

The Master said, "A gentleman can see a question from all sides
without bias. The small man* is biased and can see a question only
from one side."

---

*   Common people.

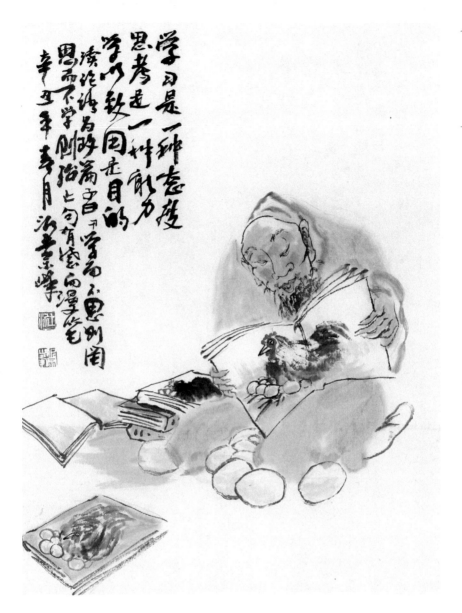

xué ér bù sī zé wǎng
学而不思则罔

zǐ yuē　　　xué ér bù sī zé wǎng　　sī ér bù xué zé dài
子曰：“学而不思则罔，思而不学则殆。”

The Master said, "He who learns but does not think is lost. He who thinks but does not learn is in great danger."

23

gōng hū yì duān

攻乎异端

zǐ yuē gōng hū yì duān sī hài yě yǐ
子曰："攻乎异端，斯害也已。"

The Master said, "He who sets to work upon a different strand
destroys the whole fabric."*

---

* The metaphor is one of weaving or netting. "Strand" is a sprout, something that sticks
out, and so "the loose end of a thread." The moral Way as opposed to the opportunist Way of
the World must be followed consistently. It is no use working at it in disconnected patches.

知之为知之
zhī zhī wéi zhī zhī

子曰："由！诲女知之乎！知之为知之，不知为不知，是知也。"

The Master said, "Yu, shall I teach you what knowledge is? When you know a thing, to recognize that you know it, and when you do not know a thing, to recognize that you do not know it. That is knowledge."

shèn xíng qí yú

慎行其余

zǐ zhāng xué gān lù　　zǐ yuē　　　duō wén quē yí　　shèn yán qí yú　　zé guǎ yóu　　duō jiàn

子张学干禄。子曰："多闻阙疑，慎言其余，则寡尤；多见

quē dài　shèn xíng qí yú　zé guǎ huǐ

阙殆，慎行其余，则寡悔。"

Tzu-chang was studying the *Song* Han-lu.* The Master said, "Hear much, but maintain silence as regards doubtful points and be cautious in speaking of the rest; then you will seldom get into trouble. See much, but ignore what is dangerous to have seen, and be cautious in acting upon the rest; then you will seldom want to undo your acts."

---

* Han-lu means "seeking princely rewards, preferment."

jǔ zhí cuò zhū wǎng
举直错诸枉

āi gōng wèn yuē　　　　　　hé wéi zé mín fú　　　　kǒng zǐ duì yuē　　　　jǔ zhí cuò zhū wǎng　　zé
哀公问曰："何为则民服？"孔子对曰："举直错诸枉，则

mín fú　　jǔ wǎng cuò zhū zhí　　　zé mín bù fú
民服；举枉错诸直，则民不服。"

Duke Ai* asked, "What can I do in order to get the support of the common people?" Master K'ung** replied, "If you raise up the straight and set them on top of the crooked, the commoners will support you. But if you raise the crooked and set them on top of the straight, the commoners will not support you."

---

* Duke of Lu.

** Confucius.

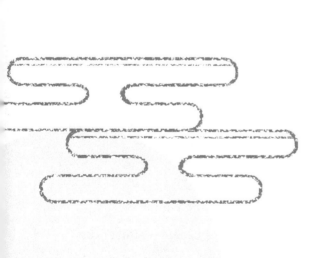

Book III

bā   yì
八佾

(Eight Rows of Dancers)

shì kě rěn yě　　　shú bù kě rěn yě
是可忍也，孰不可忍也

kǒng zǐ wèi jì shì　　　　bā yì wǔ yú tíng　　shì kě rěn yě　　shú bù kě rěn yě
孔子谓季氏："八佾舞于庭，是可忍也，孰不可忍也？"

Master K'ung said of the head of the Chi family[*] when he had eight teams of dances performing in his courtyard, "If this man can be endured, who cannot be endured!"

---

[*]　One of the Three Families that had usurped most of the powers of the Duke of Lu.

^{rén ér bù rén}   ^{rú lǐ hé}
人而不仁，如礼何

^{zǐ yuē}   ^{rén ér bù rén} ^{rú lǐ hé} ^{rén ér bù rén} ^{rú yuè hé}
子曰："人而不仁，如礼何？人而不仁，如乐何？"

The Master said, "A man who is not Good, what can he have to do with ritual? A man who is not Good, what can he have to do with music?"

The Illustrated Analects:
Selected Teachings

jūn zǐ zhī zhēng
君子之争

zǐ yuē   jūn zǐ wú suǒ zhēng   bì yě shè hū   yī ràng ér shēng   xià ér yǐn   qí zhēng
子曰："君子无所争。必也射乎！揖让而升，下而饮。其争
yě jūn zǐ
也君子。"

The Master said, "Gentlemen never compete. You will say that
in archery they do so. But even then bow and make way for one
another when they are going up to the archery-ground, when they
are coming down and at the subsequent drinking-about. Thus even
when competing, they still remain gentlemen."

君礼臣忠

dìng gōng wèn　　　　 jūn shǐ chén　 chén shì jūn　 rú zhī hé　　 kǒng zǐ duì yuē　　 jūn shǐ
定公问："君使臣，臣事君，如之何？"孔子对曰："君使
chén yǐ lǐ　 chén shì jūn yǐ zhōng
臣以礼，臣事君以忠。"

Duke Ting asked for a precept concerning a ruler's use of his ministers and a minister's service to his ruler. Master K'ung replied saying, "A ruler in employing his ministers should be guided solely by the prescriptions of ritual. Ministers in serving their ruler, solely by devotion to his cause."

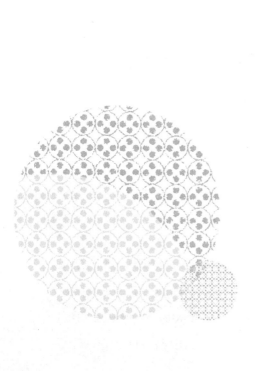

Book IV

里仁

(Benevolent Unity)

li　rén　wéi　měi
里仁为美

zǐ yuē　　　 lǐ rén wéi měi　　zé bù chǔ rén　　yān dé zhì
子曰："里仁为美。择不处仁，焉得知？"

The Master said, "It is Goodness that gives to a neighbourhood its beauty. One who is free to choose, yet does not prefer to dwell among the Good—how can he be accorded the name of wise?"

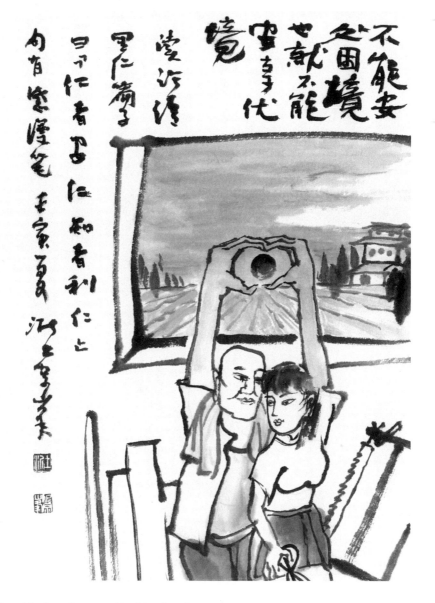

rén zhě ān rén   zhì zhě lì rén
仁者安仁，知者利仁

zǐ yuē   bù rén zhě bù kě yǐ jiǔ chǔ yuē   bù kě yǐ cháng chǔ lè   rén zhě ān rén
子曰："不仁者不可以久处约，不可以长处乐。仁者安仁，
zhì zhě lì rén
知者利仁。"

The Master said, "Without Goodness, a man cannot foe long endure

adversity, cannot for long enjoy prosperity. The Good Man rests

content with Goodness; he that is merely wise pursues Goodness in

the belief that it pays to do so."

如果有那么一天，世界上没有了善和恶，那么世界上也就没有了爱憎分明的人。读诸陆云云：「唯仁者能好人，能恶人上」句有深而浓冤。澄录峰 篆

wéi rén zhě néng hào rén
唯仁者能好人

zǐ yuē　　wéi rén zhě néng hào rén　　néng wù rén
子曰："唯仁者能好人，能恶人。"

The Master said, "Only a Good Man knows how to like people,
knows how to dislike them."

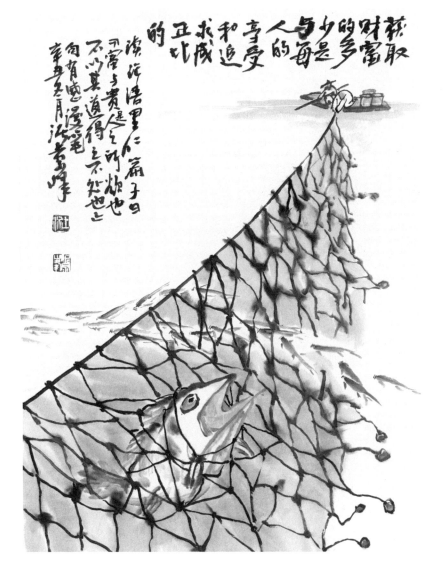

fù guì yǐ dào
富贵以道

zǐ yuē　　　　fù yǔ guì　　shì rén zhī suǒ yù yě　　bù yǐ qí dào dé zhī　bù chǔ yě
子曰："富与贵，是人之所欲也；不以其道得之，不处也。
pín yǔ jiàn　　shì rén zhī suǒ wù yě　　bù yǐ qí dào dé zhī　　bù qù yě
贫与贱，是人之所恶也；不以其道得之，不去也。"

The Master said, "Wealth and rank are what every man desires; but if they can only be retained to the detriment of the Way he professes, he must relinquish them. Poverty and obscurity are what every man detests; but if they can only be avoided to the detriment of the Way he professes, he must accept them."

错误的性质
是由犯错误
人的本质所
决定的
凝治语里仁篇
「人之过也各于其
党」句者墨居宅
冰華并翟

guān guò zhī rén
观过知仁

zǐ yuē　　　　rén zhī guò yě　　gè yú qí dǎng　guān guò　　sì zhī rén yǐ
子曰："人之过也，各于其党。观过，斯知仁矣。"

The Master said, "Every man's faults belong to a set.* If one looks
out for faults, it is only as a mean of recognizing Goodness."

---

* A set of qualities which includes virtues.

<ruby>君<rt>jūn</rt></ruby> <ruby>子<rt>zǐ</rt></ruby> <ruby>怀<rt>huái</rt></ruby> <ruby>刑<rt>xíng</rt></ruby>，<ruby>小<rt>xiǎo</rt></ruby> <ruby>人<rt>rén</rt></ruby> <ruby>怀<rt>huái</rt></ruby> <ruby>惠<rt>huì</rt></ruby>

君子怀刑，小人怀惠

子曰："君子怀德，小人怀土；君子怀刑，小人怀惠。"

The Master said, "Where gentlemen set their hearts upon moral force,* the commoners set theirs upon the soil. Where gentlemen think only of punishments, the commoners think only of exemptions."**

---

* As opposed to physical compulsion.

** Hui means amnesties, immunities, exemptions, as opposed to what is "lawful and proper."

fǎng yú lì ér xíng duō yuàn
放于利而行，多怨

zǐ yuē　　fǎng yú lì ér xíng　　duō yuàn
子曰：“放于利而行，多怨。”

The Master said, "Those[*] whose measures are dictated by mere expediency will arouse continual discontent."

---

[*]　The ruler and upper classes in general.

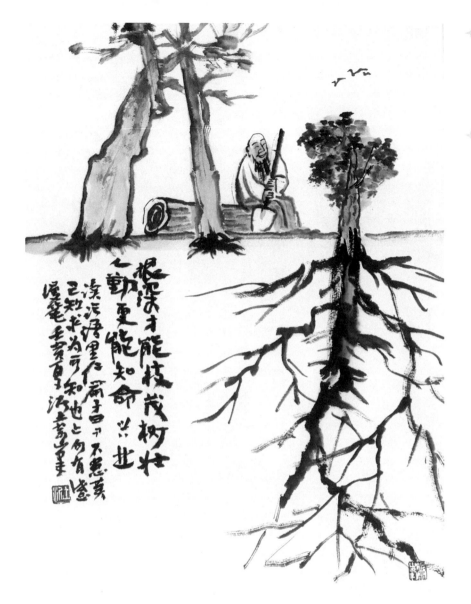

qiú   wéi   kě   zhī
求 为 可 知

zǐ yuē   bù huàn wú wèi   huàn suǒ yǐ lì   bù huàn mò jǐ zhī   qiú wéi kě zhī yě
子曰："不患无位，患所以立。不患莫己知，求为可知也。"

The Master said, "He* does not mind not being in office; all he minds about is whether he has qualities that entitle him to office. He does not mind failing to get recognition; he is too busy doing the things that entitle him to recognition."

---

* The gentleman.

以他人为鉴以观人
为镜是一个人提升
修养的根本方法

漢论语里仁篇子曰
贤思齐等见不贤而
内自省也之句有感废

寫辛丑江上李峰

jiàn xián sī qí
见贤思齐

zǐ yuē　　　　jiàn xián sī qí yān　　jiàn bù xián ér nèi zì xǐng yě
子曰："见贤思齐焉，见不贤而内自省也。"

The Master said, "In the presence of a good man, think all the time
how you may learn to equal him. In the presence of a bad man, turn
your gaze within!"

shì fù mǔ jī jiàn
事父母几谏

zǐ yuē   shì fù mǔ jī jiàn   jiàn zhì bù cóng   yòu jìng bù wéi   láo ér bù yuàn
子曰："事父母几谏，见志不从，又敬不违，劳而不怨。"

The Master said, "In serving his father and mother, a man may gently remonstrate with them. But if he sees that he has failed to change their opinion, he should resume an attitude of deference and not thwart them; may feel discouraged, but not resentful."

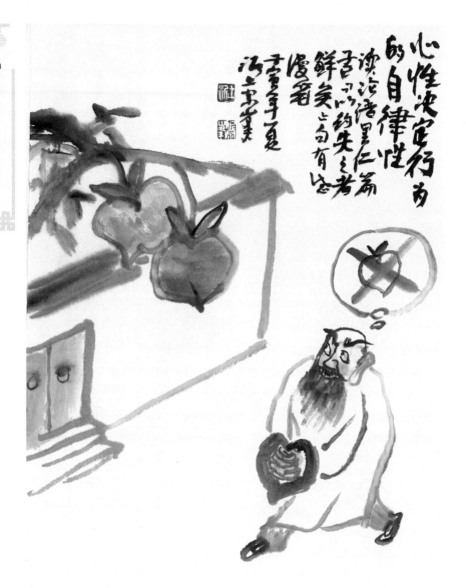

心性决定行为
的自律性

演治语里仁篇
子曰以约失之者
鲜矣之句有以念

壬寅年夏
冯之寿书

杜
正
胜

yuē zhī yǐ lǐ

约之以礼

zǐ yuē   yǐ yuē shī zhī zhě xiǎn yǐ
子曰：“以约失之者鲜矣。”

The Master said, "Those who err on the side of strictness are few
indeed!"

dé bù gū bì yǒu lín
德不孤，必有邻

zǐ yuē dé bù gū bì yǒu lín
子曰："德不孤，必有邻。"

The Master said, "Moral force never dwells in solitude; it will always

bring neighbours."*

---

* Whenever one individual or one country substitutes moral force for physical compulsion, other individuals or other countries inevitably follow suit.

Book V

gōng yě cháng
公冶长
(Gongye Chang, Son-in-Law)

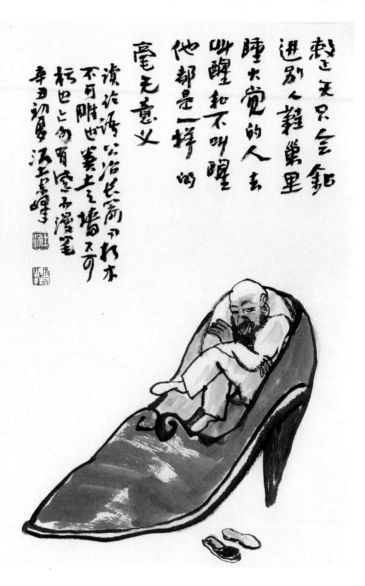

xiǔ mù bù kě diāo yě
朽木不可雕也

zǎi yú zhòu qǐn   zǐ yuē   xiǔ mù bù kě diāo yě   fèn tǔ zhī qiáng bù kě wū yě   yú
宰予昼寝。子曰："朽木不可雕也，粪土之墙不可杇也。于
yú yǔ hé zhū
予与何诛？"

Tsai Yü used to sleep during the day. The Master said, "Rotten wood cannot be carved, nor a wall of dried dung be trowelled. What use is there in my scolding him any more?"

听其言而观其行
tīng qí yán ér guān qí xíng

子曰："始吾于人也，听其言而信其行；今吾于人也，听其言而观其行。于予与改是。"

The Master said, "There was a time when I merely listened attentively to what people said, and took for granted that they would carry out their words. Now, I am obliged not only to give ear to what they say, but also to keep an eye on what they do. It was my dealings with Tsai Yü that brought about the change."

人类是在勤奋
学习中不断地完
善生存技能的。
渎论语以治
而时学不扯下问心向有月
感罗子竟 沐奎晖

mǐn ér hào xué
敏而好学

zǐ gòng wèn yuē   kǒng wén zǐ hé yǐ wèi zhī   wén   yě   zǐ yuē   mǐn ér hào
子贡问曰："孔文子何以谓之'文'也？"子曰："敏而好
xué   bù chǐ xià wèn   shì yǐ wèi zhī   wén   yě
学，不耻下问，是以谓之'文'也。"

Tzu-kung asked saying, "Why was K'ung Wên Tzu called Wên ('The
Cultured')?"* The Master said, "Because he was diligent and so fond
of learning that he was not ashamed to pick up knowledge even
from his inferiors."

---

* Why was he accorded this posthumous title?

bāng yǒu dào zé zhì
邦有道则知

zǐ yuē　　nìng wǔ zǐ　bāng yǒu dào　　zé zhì　bāng wú dào　　zé yú　　qí zhì kè jí
子曰："宁武子，邦有道，则知；邦无道，则愚。其知可及
yě　qí yú bù kě jí yě
也，其愚不可及也。"

The Master said, "Ning Wu Tzu* 'so long as the Way prevailed in his
country showed wisdom; but when the Way no longer prevailed, he
showed his folly.' To such wisdom as his we may all attain; but not
to such folly!"

---

* A minister of Wei (7th century BC), famous for his blind devotion to his prince.

lǎo zhě ān zhī
老者安之

zǐ yuē　　　　lǎo zhě ān zhī　　péng yǒu xìn zhī　　shào zhě huái zhī
子曰："老者安之，朋友信之，少者怀之。"

The Master said, "In dealing with the aged, to be comfort to them; in dealing with friends, to be of good faith with them; in dealing with the young, to cherish them."

Book VI

yōng yě
雍也

(Ran Yong,
Student of Confucius)

zhōu jí bù jì fù
周 急 不 继 富

zǐ yuē　　chì zhī shì qí yě　chéng féi mǎ　　yì qīng qiú　　wú wén zhī yě　　jūn zǐ zhōu
子曰："赤之适齐也，乘肥马，衣轻裘。吾闻之也：君子周
jí bù jì fù
急不继富。"

The Master said, "When Ch'ih[*] went to Ch'i, he drove sleek horses and was wrapped in light furs. There is a saying, 'A gentleman helps out in necessitous; he does not make the rich richer still.'"

---

[*]　Kung-hsi Hua. He ought to have left behind sufficient provision for his mother.

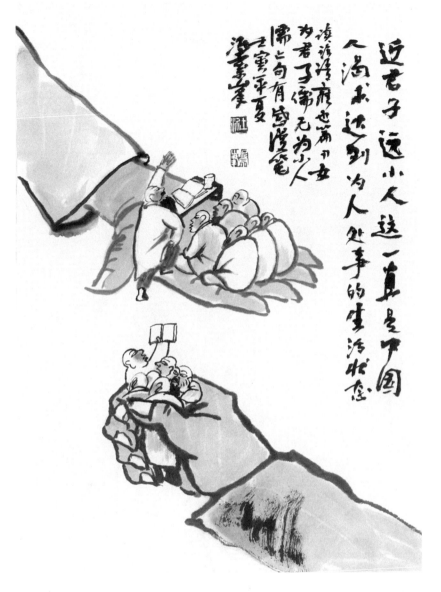

近君子 远小人 这一直是中国
人渴求 达到 为人处事的生活水准

读论语 雍也篇 �女
为君子儒 无为小人
儒也句有道理图
壬寅平夏
游寄生笔

wéi jūn zǐ rú
为君子儒

zǐ wèi zǐ xià yuē   rǔ wéi jūn zǐ rú   wú wéi xiǎo rén rú
子谓子夏曰："女为君子儒，无为小人儒。

The Master said to Tzu-hsia, "You must practise the *ju** of gentle-men, not that of the common people."

---

* A word of very uncertain meaning. Perhaps "unwarlikeness." The meaning of the saying may be "The unwarlikeness of gentlemen means a preference for moral force, that of inferior people is mere cowardice."

wén zhì bīn bīn　　rán hòu jūn zǐ

文质彬彬，然后君子

zǐ yuē　　　zhì shèng wén zé yě　wén shèng zhì zé shǐ　wén zhì bīn bīn　　rán hòu jūn zǐ

子曰："质胜文则野，文胜质则史。文质彬彬，然后君子。"

The Master said, "When natural substance prevails over ornamentation,* you get the boorishness of the rustic. When ornamentation prevails over natural substance, you get the pedantry of the scribe. Only when ornament of substance are duly blended do you get the true gentleman."

---

* When nature prevails over culture.

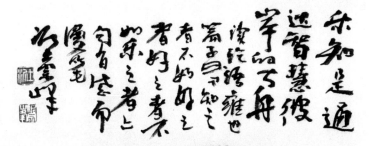

_{zhī zhī} _{hào zhī} _{lè zhī}
知之、好之、乐之

_{zǐ yuē} _{zhī zhī zhě bù rú hào zhī zhě} _{hào zhī zhě bù rú lè zhī zhě}
子曰：“知之者不如好之者，好之者不如乐之者。”

The Master said, "To prefer it* is better than only to know it. To delight in it is better than merely to prefer it."

---

* The Way.

jìng guǐ shén ér yuǎn zhī
敬鬼神而远之

fán chí wèn zhì   zǐ yuē   wù mín zhī yì   jìng guǐ shén ér yuǎn zhī   kě wèi zhì yǐ
樊迟问知。子曰："务民之义，敬鬼神而远之，可谓知矣。"

Fan Ch'ih asked about wisdom.* The Master said, "He who devotes
himself to securing for his subjects what it is right they should have,
who by respect for the Spirits** keeps them at a distance, may be
termed wise."

---

* To what rulers the title "Wise" could be accorded.

** When the Spirits of hills and streams do not receive their proper share of ritual and
sacrifice, they do not "keep their distance," but "posses" human beings, causing madness,
sickness, pestilence, etc.

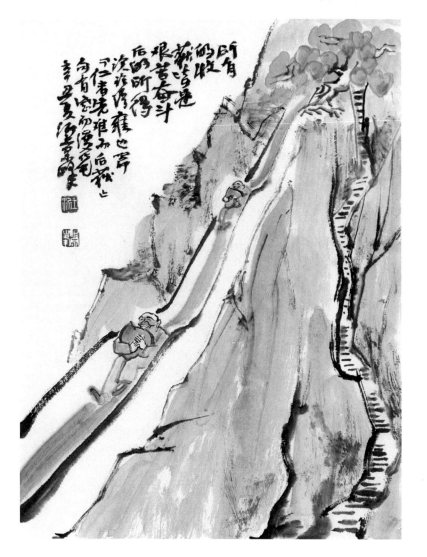

xiān nán ér hòu huò

先难而后获

wèn rén yuē rén zhě xiān nán ér hòu huò kě wèi rén yǐ

问仁。曰："仁者先难而后获，可谓仁矣。"

He[*] asked about Goodness. The Master said, "Goodness cannot be obtained till what is difficult has been truly done. He who has done this may be called Good."

---

[*] Fan Ch'ih.

lè shuǐ lè shān
乐水乐山

zǐ yuē　　zhì zhě yào shuǐ　rén zhě yào shān　zhì zhě dòng　rén zhě jìng　zhì zhě lè
子曰："知者乐水，仁者乐山。知者动，仁者静。知者乐，
rén zhě shòu
仁者寿。"

The Master said, "The wise man delights in water, the Good man delights in mountains. For the wise move; but the Good stay still. The wise are happy; but the Good, secure."

人的寿命是有限的，仁者的精神是无限的。淡泊宁静，也而寿，者乐，仁者寿之句有密切笔致。辛丑冬月 汪念羆

知者乐，仁者寿
zhì zhě lè　rén zhě shòu

子曰：“知者乐水，仁者乐山。知者动，仁者静。知者乐，仁者寿。”
zǐ yuē　　zhì zhě yào shuǐ　rén zhě yào shān　zhì zhě dòng　rén zhě jìng　zhì zhě lè　rén zhě shòu

The Master said, "The wise man delights in water, the Good man delights in mountains. For the wise move; but the Good stay still. The wise are happy; but the Good, secure."

^{kě} ^{qī} ^{yě}　　^{bù} ^{kě} ^{wǎng} ^{yě}
可 欺 也，不 可 罔 也

^{zǐ} ^{yuē}　　　^{jūn} ^{zǐ} ^{kě} ^{shì} ^{yě}　　^{bù} ^{kě} ^{xiàn} ^{yě}　　^{kě} ^{qī} ^{yě}　　^{bù} ^{kě} ^{wǎng} ^{yě}
子曰："君子可逝也，不可陷也；可欺也，不可罔也。"

The Master said, "A gentleman can be broken,* but cannot be dented; may be deceived, but cannot be led astray."**

---

* The gentleman (like jade) can be broken, but not bent.

** Deceived as to facts; but cannot be enticed into wrong conduct.

中庸不只是讲不
走中间的道，而
是讲选择走符
合规律的路
涤华海巴他也等
子曰"中庸之
为德也上有途而
漫笔海巴也峰

zhōng yōng wéi dé
中庸为德

zǐ yuē　　zhōng yōng zhī wéi dé yě　　qí zhì yǐ hū　　mín xiǎn jiǔ yǐ
子曰："中庸之为德也，其至矣乎！民鲜久矣。"

The Master said, "How transcendent is the moral power of the Middle Use!* That it is but rarely found among the common people is a face long admitted."

---

* Confucius's Way was essentially one of moderation: "To exceed is as bad as to fall short."

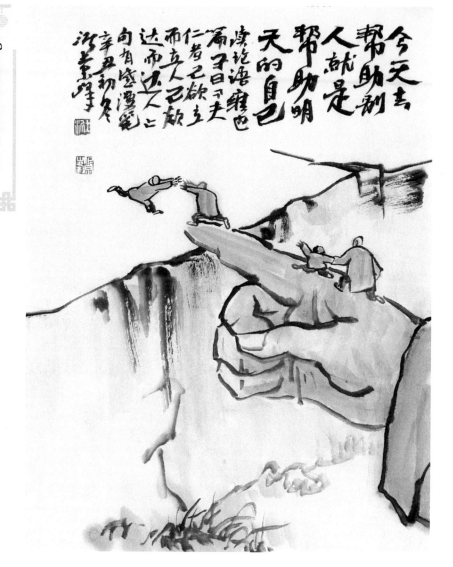

jǐ yù lì ér lì rén　　jǐ yù dá ér dá rén
己欲立而立人，已欲达而达人

zǐ yuē　　　fú rén zhě　　jǐ yù lì ér lì rén　　jǐ yù dá ér dá rén　　néng jìn qǔ
子曰："夫仁者，已欲立而立人，已欲达而达人。能近取
pì　　kě wèi rén zhī fāng yě yǐ
譬，可谓仁之方也已。"

The Master said, "As for Goodness—you yourself desire rank and standing; then help others to get rank and standing. You want to turn your own merits to account; then help others to turn theirs to account— in fact, the ability to take one's own feeling as a guide— that is the sort of thing that lies in the direction of Goodness."

Book VII

述 而 (Transmission)

xué ér bù yàn　　huì rén bù juàn
学而不厌，诲人不倦

zǐ yuē　　　　mò ér zhì zhī　xué ér bù yàn　huì rén bù juàn　　hé yǒu yú wǒ zāi
子曰："默而识之，学而不厌，诲人不倦，何有于我哉？"

The Master said, "I have listened in silence and noted what was said, I have never grown tired of learning nor wearied of teaching others what I have learnt. These at least are merits which I can confidently claim."

zhì dào yóu yì
志道游艺

zǐ yuē zhì yú dào jù yú dé yī yú rén yóu yú yì
子曰："志于道，据于德，依于仁，游于艺。"

The Master said, "Set your heart upon the Way, support yourself by its power, learn upon Goodness, seek distraction in the arts."*

---

* Music, archery, and the like.

69

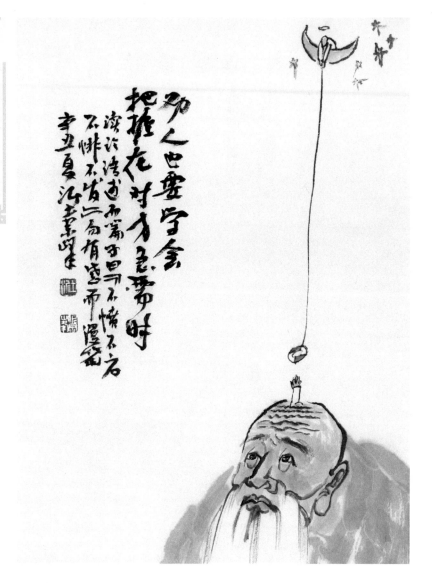

bù fèn bù qǐ bù fěi bù fā

不愤不启，不悱不发

zǐ yuē bù fèn bù qǐ bù fěi bù fā

子曰："不愤不启，不悱不发。

The Master said, "Only one who bursts with eagerness do I instruct;

only one who bubbles with excitement, do I enlighten."

hào móu ér chéng
好 谋 而 成

zǐ yuē　　　 bào hǔ píng hé　　 sǐ ér wú huǐ zhě　　 wú bù yǔ yě　　 bì yě lín shì ér
子曰："暴虎冯河，死而无悔者，吾不与也。必也临事而
jù　 hào móu ér chéng zhě yě
惧，好谋而成者也。"

The Master said, "The man who was ready to 'beard a tiger or rush a river' without caring whether he lived or died—that sort of man I should not take. I should certainly take someone who approached difficulties with due caution and who preferred to succeed by strategy."

bù yì ér fù qiě guì　　yú wǒ rú fú yún
不义而富且贵，于我如浮云

zǐ yuē　　　　fàn shū shí yǐn shuǐ　　qū gōng ér zhěn zhī　　lè yì zài qí zhōng yǐ　　bù yì ér
子曰："饭疏食饮水，曲肱而枕之，乐亦在其中矣。不义而
fù qiě guì　　yú wǒ rú fú yún
富且贵，于我如浮云。"

The Master said, "He who seeks only coarse food to eat, water to drink and a bent arm for pillow, will without looking for it find happiness to boot. Any thought of accepting wealth and rank by means that I know to be wring is as remote from me as the clouds that float above."

lè yǐ wàng yōu
乐以忘忧

shè gōng wèn kǒng zǐ yú zǐ lù   zǐ lù bù duì   zǐ yuē   rǔ xī bù yuē   qí wéi rén
叶公问孔子于子路，子路不对。子曰："女奚不曰，其为人
yě   fā fèn wàng shí   lè yǐ wàng yōu   bù zhī lǎo zhī jiāng zhì yún ěr
也，发愤忘食，乐以忘忧，不知老之将至云尔。"

The Duke of Shê* asked Tzu-lu about Master K'ung (Confucius).
Tzu-lu did not reply. The Master said, "Why did you not say 'This is
the character of the man: so intent upon enlightening the eager that
he forgets his hunger, and so happy in doing so, that he forgets the
bitterness of his lot and does not realize that old age is at hand.'**
That is what he is."

---

* Shen Chu-liang (c. 550–c. 470 BC) was a general and Prime Minister of the Kingdom of
Chu. After his father's death, King Zhao of Chu enfeoffed Shen Chu-liang. with the city of
Shê, so he was known as Duke of Shê.

** According to the traditional chronology, Confucius was sixty-two at the time when this
was said.

fēi shēng ér zhī zhī

非生而知之

zǐ yuē　　　wǒ fēi shēng ér zhī zhī zhě　　hào gǔ　　mǐn yǐ qiú zhī zhě yě

子曰："我非生而知之者，好古，敏以求之者也。"

The Master said, "I for my part am not one of those who have innate knowledge. I am simply one who loves the past and who is diligent in investigating it."

多人走在路上走得母与走得

环走由自己把握

演得淺过而扁行三人行必有我师学

句有密度笔辛丑夏沈幸拳

^{sān rén xíng} ^{bì yǒu wǒ shī}
三人行，必有我师

^{zǐ yuē} ^{sān rén xíng} ^{bì yǒu wǒ shī yān} ^{zé qí shàn zhě ér cóng zhī} ^{qí bù shàn zhě}
子曰："三人行，必有我师焉。择其善者而从之，其不善者
^{ér gǎi zhī}
而改之。"

The Master said, "Even when walking in a party of no more than three, I can always be certain of learning from those I am with. There will be good qualities that I can select for imitation and bad ones that will teach me what requires correction in myself."

duō jiàn ér zhì
多见而识

zǐ yuē　　　　gài yǒu bù zhī ér zuò zhī zhě　　wǒ wú shì yě　　duō wén　　zé qí shàn zhě ér
子曰："盖有不知而作之者，我无是也。多闻，择其善者而

cóng zhī　　　duō jiàn ér zhì zhī　　　zhī zhī cì yě
从之；多见而识之；知之次也。"

The Master said, "There may well be those who can do without

knowledge; but I for my part am certainly not one of them. To hear

much, pick out what is good and follow it, to see much and take due

note of it, is the lower* of the two kinds of knowledge.

---

* The higher being innate knowledge.

_{wǒ yù rén   sī rén zhì yǐ}
我欲仁，斯仁至矣

_{zǐ yuē   rén yuǎn hū zāi   wǒ yù rén   sī rén zhì yǐ}
子曰："仁远乎哉？我欲仁，斯仁至矣。"

The Master said, "Is Goodness indeed so far away? If we really wanted Goodness, we should find that it was at our very side."

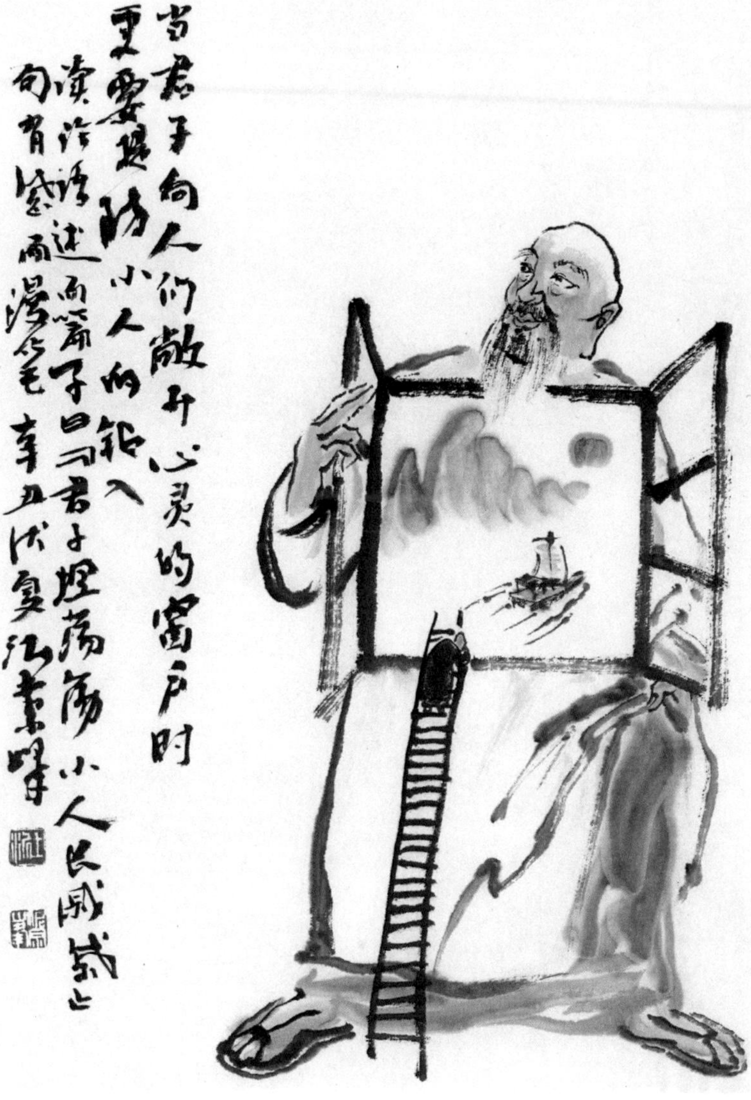

当君子向人们敞开心灵的窗户时
更要提防小人的钻入
演沂诗述而篇子曰君子坦荡荡小人长戚戚
句首涂雨漫今毛辛丑夏江业哗

jūn zǐ tǎn dàng dàng   xiǎo rén cháng qī qī
君 子 坦 荡 荡， 小 人 长 戚 戚

zǐ yuē   jūn zǐ tǎn dàng dàng   xiǎo rén cháng qī qī
子曰："君子坦荡荡，小人长戚戚。"

The Master said, "The true gentlemen is calm and at ease; the small
man is fretful and ill at ease."

Book VIII

tài bó
泰伯
(Wu Taibo,
Founder of the State of Chu)

rèn zhòng dào yuǎn

任重道远

zēng zǐ yuē   shì bù kě yǐ bù hóng yì   rèn zhòng ér dào yuǎn   rén yǐ wéi jǐ rèn

曾子曰："士不可以不弘毅，任重而道远。仁以为己任，

bù yì zhòng hū   sǐ ér hòu yǐ   bù yì yuǎn hū

不亦重乎？死而后已，不亦远乎？"

Master Tsêng said, "The true Knight of the Way must perforce be
both broad-shouldered and stout of heart; his burden is heavy and
he has far to go. For Goodness is the burden he has taken upon
himself; and must we not grant that it is a heavy one to bear? Only
with death does his journey end; then must we not grant that he
has far to go?"

rén ér bù rén jí zhī yǐ shèn luàn yě
人而不仁，疾之已甚，乱也

zǐ yuē   rén ér bù rén   jí zhī yǐ shèn   luàn yě
子曰："人而不仁，疾之已甚，乱也。"

The Master said, "Indeed, any men, save those that are truly Good,

if their sufferings are very great, will be likely rebel."*

---

* Official interpretation, "Men who are not truly Good, if you criticize them too severely, are likely to rebel."

bāng yǒu dào   pín qiě jiàn yān   chǐ yě

邦有道，贫且贱焉，耻也

zǐ yuē   tiān xià yǒu dào zé xiàn   wú dào zé yǐn   bāng yǒu dào   pín qiě jiàn yān   chǐ
子曰："天下有道则见，无道则隐。邦有道，贫且贱焉，耻
yě bāng wú dào   fù qiě guì yān   chǐ yě
也；邦无道，富且贵焉，耻也。"

The Master said, "When the Way prevails under Heaven, then show
yourself; when it does not prevail, then hide. When the Way prevails
in your own land, count it a disgrace to be needy and obscure; when
the Way does not prevail in your land, then count it a disgrace to be
rich and honoured."

bù zài qí wèi　bù móu qí zhèng
不在其位，不谋其政

zǐ yuē　bù zài qí wèi　bù móu qí zhèng
子曰："不在其位，不谋其政。"

The Master said, "He who holds no rank in a State does not discuss its policies."

xué rú bù jí yóu kǒng shī zhī
学如不及，犹恐失之

zǐ yuē xué rú bù jí yóu kǒng shī zhī
子曰："学如不及，犹恐失之。"

The Master said, "Learn as if you were following someone whom you could not catch up, as though it were someone you were frighted of losing."

Book IX

子 罕

(The Master Shunned)

牯一个人没有能力在官
场上混事，就一定要学门
技艺因来寄家糊口
读此语子军篇牢曰子云
吾不试故艺也句有墨存
溪宽书乙太夏
汪曹峰

wú bù shì　gù yì
吾不试，故艺

láo yuē　zǐ yún　　wú bù shì　gù yì
牢曰：“子云：‘吾不试，故艺。’”

Lao says that the Master said, "It is because I have not been given a
chance that I have become so handy."

人們能尋得住河岸
卻留不住湍急的河流
讀淪語至牢而
以上句逝者如斯夫
不舍晝夜之句有感
漫筆治畫筆

shì zhě rú sī fū
逝者如斯夫

zǐ zài chuān shàng   yuē   shì zhě rú sī fū   bù shě zhòu yè
子在川上，曰："逝者如斯夫！不舍晝夜。"

Once when the Master was standing by a steam, he said, "Could one but go on and on like this, never ceasing day or night!"

hòu shēng kě wèi
后生可畏

zǐ yuē　　hòu shēng kě wèi　　yān zhī lái zhě zhī bù rú jīn yě　　sì shí　　wǔ shí ér
子曰："后生可畏，焉知来者之不如今也？四十、五十而
wú wén yān　　sī yì bù zú wèi yě yǐ
无闻焉，斯亦不足畏也已。"

The Master said, "Respect the young. How do you know that they will not one day be all that you are now? But if a man has reached forty or fifty and nothing has been heard of him, then I grant there is no need to respect him."

人们应不应意意
听其讲
话是听话人判断
讲话人德们的
标准

读论语于字岩
子曰法语之言
能无从乎攻之
沟贵之句有慈
而慢笔辛丑伏
夏沐志永峰

fǎ yǔ zhī yán　　néng wú cóng hū

法语之言，能无从乎

zǐ yuē　　　fǎ yǔ zhī yán　　néng wú cóng hū　　gǎi zhī wéi guì　　xùn yǔ zhī yán　　néng wú

子曰："法语之言，能无从乎？改之为贵。巽与之言，能无

yuè hū　　yì zhī wéi guì

说乎？绎之为贵。"

The Master said, "The words of the *Fa Yü*[*] cannot fail to stir us;
but what matters is that they should change our ways. The words
of *Hsüan Chü*[**] cannot fail to commend themselves to us; but what
matters is that we should carry them out."

---

[*] Words that are in accordance with the principles of etiquette and law.

[**] Words of obedience and approval.

pǐ fū bù kě duó zhì yě
匹夫不可夺志也

zǐ yuē　　　　sān jūn kě duó shuài yě　　pǐ fū bù kě duó zhì yě
子曰："三军可夺帅也，匹夫不可夺志也。"

The Master said, "You may rob the Three Armies of their commander-in-chief, but you cannot deprive the humblest peasant of his opinion."

suì hán zhī sōng bǎi

岁寒知松柏

zǐ yuē suì hán rán hòu zhī sōng bǎi zhī hòu diāo yě

子曰："岁寒，然后知松柏之后凋也。"

The Master said, "Only when the year grows could do we see that pine and cypress are the last to fade."

Book X

xiāng dǎng

乡党

(The Xiang and
Dang Clans)

<small>shí bù yǔ   qǐn bù yán</small>
食不语，寝不言

<small>shí bù yǔ   qǐn bù yán</small>
食不语，寝不言。

While it is being eaten, there must be no conversation, nor any word spoken while lying down after the repast.

人是创造社会的根本如果没有了人
就没有了劳动

读论语多觉而
偶人才不问马也
辛丑年夏
汉城三老学

wèn rén bù wèn mǎ
问人不问马

jiù fén　　zǐ tuì cháo　　yuē　　shāng rén hū　　bù wèn mǎ
厩焚。子退朝，曰："伤人乎？"不问马。

When the stables were burnt down, on returning from Court, he said, "Was anyone hurt?" He did not ask about the horses.

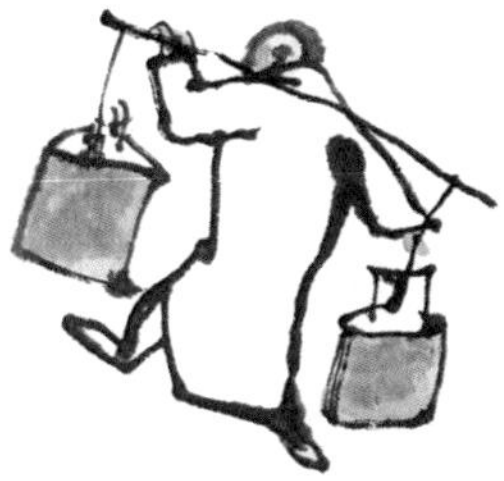

Book XI

xiān jìn
先进
(Former Generations)

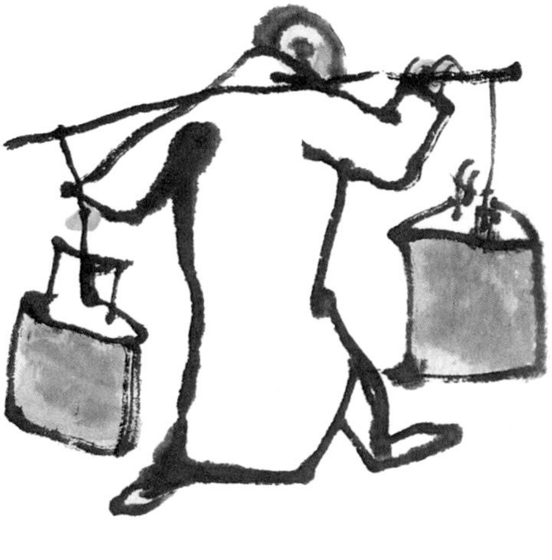

wèi zhī shēng， yān zhī sǐ
未知生，焉知死

jì lù wèn shì guǐ shén zǐ yuē   wèi néng shì rén   yān néng shì guǐ   yuē   gǎn
季路问事鬼神。子曰："未能事人，焉能事鬼？"曰："敢
wèn sǐ   yuē   wèi zhī shēng yān zhī sǐ
问死。"曰："未知生，焉知死？"

Tzu-lu asked how one should serve ghosts and spirits. The Master said, "Till you have learnt to serve men, how can you serve ghosts?" Tzu-lu then ventured upon a question about the dead. The Master said, "Till you know about the living, how are you to know about the dead?"

yán bì yǒu zhòng
言必有中

lǔ rén wéi zhǎng fǔ   mǐn zǐ qiān yuē   réng jiù guàn   rú zhī hé   hé bì gǎi zuò
鲁人为长府。闵子骞曰："仍旧贯，如之何？何必改作？"
zǐ yuē   fú rén bù yán   yán bì yǒu zhòng
子曰："夫人不言，言必有中。"

When the men of Lu were dealing with the question of the Long Treasury, Min Tzu-ch'ien said, "What about restoring it on the old lines? I see no necessity for rebuilding it on a new plan." The Master said, "That man is no talker; but when he does say anything, he invariably hits the mark."

99

bù jiàn jì   yì bù rù yú shì
不 践 迹， 亦 不 入 于 室

zǐ zhāng wèn shàn rén zhī dào   zǐ yuē   bù jiàn jì   yì bù rù yú shì
子 张 问 善 人 之 道。 子 曰： "不 践 迹， 亦 不 入 于 室。"

Tzu-chang asked about the Way of the good people. The Master
said, "He who does not tread in the tracks* cannot expect to find his
way into the Inner Room."

---

* Of the Ancients.

Book XII

yán yuān
颜 渊 (Yan Yuan,
Disciple of Confucius)

kè jǐ fù lǐ wéi rén

克己复礼为仁

yán yuān wèn rén zǐ yuē kè jǐ fù lǐ wéi rén

颜渊问仁。子曰：“克己复礼为仁。”

Yen Hui asked about Goodness. The Master said, “He who can himself submit to ritual is Good.”

wéi rén yóu jǐ
为仁由己

zǐ yuē　　　wéi rén yóu jǐ　　ér yóu rén hū zāi
子曰："为仁由己，而由人乎哉？"

The Master said, "For Goodness is something that must have its source in the ruler himself; it cannot be got from others."

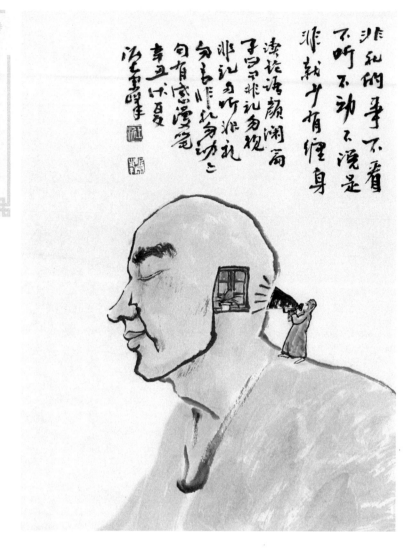

fēi lǐ wù yán   fēi lǐ wù dòng
非礼勿言，非礼勿动

zǐ yuē   fēi lǐ wù shì   fēi lǐ wù tīng   fēi lǐ wù yán   fēi lǐ wù dòng
子曰："非礼勿视，非礼勿听，非礼勿言，非礼勿动。"

The Master said, "To look at nothing in defiance of ritual, to listen to nothing in defiance of ritual, to speak of nothing in defiance of ritual, never to stir hand or foot in defiance of ritual."

己所不欲，勒施于人（著者題字）
子曰己所不欲
勿施于人之句有
盛漫笔 辛丑李
秋 泾生泽峰

自己不想接别人
别去限制别人禁铜那就
读论语颜渊篇

jǐ suǒ bù yù　　wù shī yú rén
己所不欲，勿施于人

zhòng gōng wèn rén　　zǐ yuē　　chū mén rú jiàn dà bīn　　shǐ mín rú chéng dà jì　　jǐ suǒ
仲 弓 问 仁。子曰："出门如见大宾，使民如承大祭。己所
bù yù　　wù shī yú rén
不欲，勿施于人。"

Jan Jung asked about Goodness.* The Master said, "Behave when away from home as though you were in the presence of an important guest. Deal with the common people ads though you were officiating at an important sacrifice. Do not do to others what you would not like yourself."

---

* Ruling by Goodness, not by force.

見波瀾心不惊 岂由子不因外物 毋环和自己得失而喜或悲 读论语颜渊而子曰内省不疚夫行 忧何惧之句有它漫笔 辛丑年仲夏沙里斋峰 (seals)

nèi xǐng bù jiù
内省不疚

sī mǎ niú wèn jūn zǐ   zǐ yuē   jūn zǐ bù yōu bù jù   yuē   bù yōu bù
司马牛问君子。子曰: "君子不忧不惧。"曰: "不忧不
jù   sī wèi zhī jūn zǐ yǐ hū   zǐ yuē   nèi xǐng bù jiù   fú hé yōu hé jù
惧, 斯谓之君子已乎? "子曰: "内省不疚, 夫何忧何惧? "

Ssu-ma Niu[*] asked about Goodness. The Master said, "The Good
man is chary of speech." Ssu-ma Niu said, "So that is what is meant
by Goodness—to be chary of speech?" The Master said, "Seeing that
the doing of it is so difficult, how can one be otherwise than chary
of talking about it?"

---

* A great talker and a native of Song.

sì hǎi zhī nèi jiē xiōng dì
四海之内皆兄弟

zǐ xià yuē　　　　shāng wén zhī yǐ　　sǐ shēng yǒu mìng　　fù guì zài tiān　　jūn zǐ jìng ér wú
子夏曰："商闻之矣：死生有命，富贵在天。君子敬而无
shī　　yǔ rén gōng ér yǒu lǐ　　sì hǎi zhī nèi　　jiē xiōng dì yě　　jūn zǐ hé huàn hū wú
失，与人恭而有礼，四海之内，皆兄弟也。君子何患乎无
xiōng dì yě
兄弟也？"

Tzu-hsia said, "I have heard this saying, 'Death and life are the decree of Heaven; wealth and rank depend upon the will of Heaven. If a gentleman attends to business and does not idle away his time, if he behaves with courtesy to others and observes the rules of ritual, then all within the Four Seas[*] are his brothers.' How can any true gentleman grieve that he is without brothers?"

---

[*] That bound the universe.

jū zhī wú juàn   xíng zhī yǐ zhōng
居之无倦，行之以忠

zǐ zhāng wèn zhèng   zǐ yuē   jū zhī wú juàn   xíng zhī yǐ zhōng
子张问政。子曰："居之无倦，行之以忠。"

Tzu-chang asked about public business. The Master said, "Ponder over it untiringly at home; carry it out loyally when the times comes."*

---

*   Literally, "Home it untiringly, carry it out loyalty."

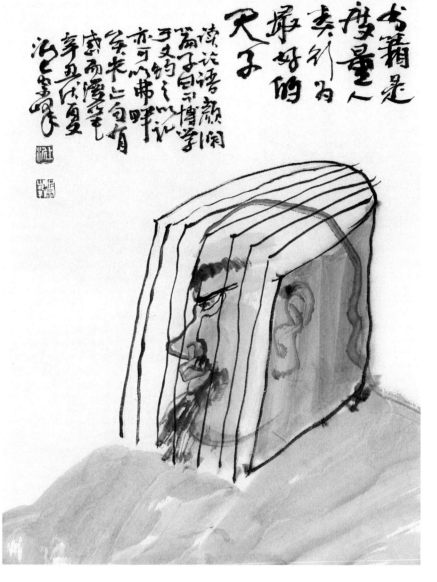

^{bó} ^{xué} ^{yú} ^{wén}　　　^{yuē} ^{zhī} ^{yǐ} ^{lǐ}
博 学 于 文， 约 之 以 礼

^{zǐ} ^{yuē}　　　 ^{bó} ^{xué} ^{yú} ^{wén}　　 ^{yuē} ^{zhī} ^{yǐ} ^{lǐ}　　 ^{yì} ^{kě} ^{yǐ} ^{fú} ^{pàn} ^{yǐ} ^{fú}
子曰：“博学于文， 约之以礼， 亦可以弗畔矣夫！”

The Master said, "A gentleman who is widely versed in letters and at the same time knows how to submit his learning to the restraints of ritual is not likely, I think, to go far wrong."

chéng rén zhī měi
成人之美

zǐ yuē　　jūn zǐ chéng rén zhī měi　　bù chéng rén zhī è　　xiǎo rén fǎn shì
子曰：“君子成人之美，不成人之恶。小人反是。”

The Master said, "The gentlemen calls attention to the good points in others; he does not call attention to their defects. The small man does just the reverse of this."

命令只能去指使人身
传力行才能带动人

澜洺诗颜涮篇『政者已
也子帅以丘孰敢不正と
句有憲恩聋笔泫素学墓

zhèng zhě zhèng yě
政者正也

jì kāng zǐ wèn zhèng yú kǒng zǐ   kǒng zǐ duì yuē   zhèng zhě   zhèng yě   zǐ shuài yǐ zhèng
季康子问政于孔子。孔子对曰："政者，正也。子帅以正，
shú gǎn bù zhèng
孰敢不正？"

Chi K'anf-tzu asked Master K'ung about the art of ruling. Master

K'ung said, "Ruling is straightening. If you lead long a straight way,

who will dare go by a crooked one?"

jūn zǐ dé fēng
君子德风

kǒng zǐ duì yuē   zǐ wéi zhèng   yān yòng shā   zǐ yù shàn ér mín shàn yǐ   jūn zǐ zhī dé
孔子对曰："子为政，焉用杀？子欲善而民善矣。君子之德
fēng   xiǎo rén zhī dé cǎo   cǎo shàng zhī fēng   bì yǎn
风，小人之德草，草上之风，必偃。"

Master K'ung replied saying, "You are there to rule, not to slay.
If you desire what is good, the people will at once be good. The
essence of the gentleman is that of wind; the essence of small
people is that of grass. And when a wind passes over the grass, it
cannot choose but bend."

^{zhì} ^{zhí} ^{ér} ^{hào} ^{yì}
质直而好义

^{zǐ} ^{yuē}   ^{fú} ^{dá} ^{yě} ^{zhě}   ^{zhì} ^{zhí} ^{ér} ^{hào} ^{yì}   ^{chá} ^{yán} ^{ér} ^{guān} ^{sè}   ^{lǜ} ^{yǐ} ^{xià} ^{rén}
子曰："夫达也者，质直而好义，察言而观色，虑以下人。"

The Master said, "In order to be influential, a man must be by nature straight-forward and a lover of right. He must examine men's words and observe their expressions, and bear in mind the necessity of deferring to others."

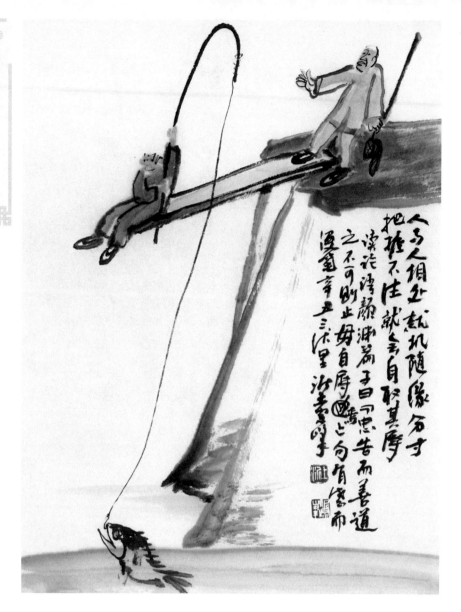

The Illustrated Analects:
Selected Teachings

zhōng gào shàn dào
忠告善道

zǐ gòng wèn yǒu   zǐ yuē   zhōng gào ér shàn dào zhī   bù kě zé zhǐ   wú zì rǔ yān
子贡问友。子曰："忠告而善道之，不可则止，毋自辱焉。"

Tzu-kung asked about friend. The Master said, "Inform them loyally and guide them discreetly. If that fails, then desist. Do not court humiliation."

yǐ wén huì yǒu

以文会友

zēng zǐ yuē   jūn zǐ yǐ wén huì yǒu   yǐ yǒu fǔ rén

曾子曰: "君子以文会友, 以友辅仁。"

Master Tsêng said, "The gentleman by his culture collects friends about him, and through these friends promotes Goodness."

Book XIII

子路

(Zi Lu,
Student of Confucius)

xiān zhī láo zhī
先之劳之

zǐ lù wèn zhèng　　zǐ yuē　　xiān zhī láo zhī　　qǐng yì　　yuē　　wú juàn
子路问政。子曰："先之劳之。"请益。曰："无倦。"

Tzu-lu asked about government. The Master said, "Lead them; encourage them!" Tzu-lu asked for a further maxim. The Master said, "Untiringly."

jǔ ěr suǒ zhī
举尔所知

zǐ yuē　　jǔ ěr suǒ zhī　ěr suǒ bù zhī　rén qí shě zhū
子曰："举尔所知；尔所不知，人其舍诸？"

The Master said, "Promote those you know, and those whom you do not know other people will certainly not neglect."*

---

* Will certainly bring to your notice.

míng zhèng yán shùn

名正言顺

子曰："名不正则言不顺；言不顺则事不成；事不成则礼乐不兴；礼乐不兴则刑罚不中；刑罚不中则民无所措手足。"

The Master said, "If language is incorrect, then what is said does not concord with what was meant; and if what is said does not concord with what was meant, what is to be done cannot be effected. If what is to be done cannot be effected, then rites and music will not flourish. If rites and music do not flourish, then mutilations and lesser punishments will go astray. And if mutilations and lesser punishments go astray, then the people have nowhere to put hand or foot."

qí shēn zhèng　　bù lìng ér xíng
其身正，不令而行

zǐ yuē　　qí shēn zhèng　　bù lìng ér xíng　　qí shēn bù zhèng　　suī lìng bù cóng
子曰：“其身正，不令而行；其身不正，虽令不从。”

The Master said, "If the ruler himself ids upright, all will go well even though he does not give orders. But if he himself is not upright, even though he gives orders, they will not be obeyed."

jìn yuè yuǎn lái
近说远来

shè gōng wèn zhèng　　zǐ yuē　　　jìn zhě yuè　　yuǎn zhě lái
叶公问政。子曰:"近者说,远者来。"

The Duke of Shê asked about government. The Master said, "When the near approve and the distant approach."

yù sù zé bù dá
欲速则不达

zǐ xià wéi jǔ fù zǎi　　wèn zhèng　　zǐ yuē　　　　wú yù sù　　wú jiàn xiǎo lì　　yù sù
子夏为莒父宰，问政。子曰："无欲速，无见小利。欲速，
zé bù dá　　jiàn xiǎo lì　　zé dà shì bù chéng
则不达；见小利，则大事不成。"

When Tzu-hsia was Warden of Chü-fu,[*] he asked for advice about government. The Master said, "Do not try to hurry things. Ignore minor considerations. If you hurry thins, your personality will not come into play. If you let yourself be distracted by minor considerations, nothing important will ever get finished."

---

[*] A town in Lu.

hé ér bù tóng
和而不同

zǐ yuē　　　jūn zǐ hé ér bù tóng　　xiǎo rén tóng ér bù hé
子曰："君子和而不同，小人同而不和。"

The Master said, "The true gentleman is conciliatory but not accommodating. Common people are accommodating but not conciliatory."*

---

* "Accommodating" means ready to sacrifice principles to agreement.

<ruby>善 zhě<rt>shàn</rt></ruby>

善者好之，其不善恶之
shàn zhě hào zhī　　qí bù shàn wù zhī

"乡人皆恶之，何如？" 子曰: "未可也。不如乡人之善者
好之，其不善者恶之。"
xiāng rén jiē wù zhī　　hé rú　　zǐ yuē　　wèi kě yě　　bù rú xiāng rén zhī shàn zhě
hào zhī　　qí bù shàn zhě wù zhī

"What would you feel about a man who was hated by all his fellow-villagers?" The Master said, "That is not enough. Best of all would be that the good people in his village loved him and the bad hated him."

125

jūn zǐ yì shì ér nán yuè yě

君子易事而难说也

zǐ yuē　　jūn zǐ yì shì ér nán yuè yě

子曰："君子易事而难说也。"

The Master said, "The true gentleman is easy to serve, yet difficult to please."

Book XIV

宪问

(Yuan Xian,
Student of Confucius)

shì bù huái jū
士不怀居

zǐ yuē　　shì ér huái jū　　bù zú yǐ wéi shì yǐ
子曰："士而怀居，不足以为士矣。"

The Master said, "The knight of the Way who thinks only of sitting quietly at home is not worthy to be called a knight."

好人一定会论
士好考的活
但是能说好
听话的不一定都
是好人

遵照唐宽白满
子曰二句有儌书以
不里有言者必
慼澄笔
一句有德
辛丑仲秋
江叟郁虹

yǒu dé zhě bì yǒu yán
有德者必有言

zǐ yuē　　yǒu dé zhě bì yǒu yán　yǒu yán zhě bù bì yǒu dé　rén zhě bì yǒu yǒng　yǒng
子曰："有德者必有言，有言者不必有德。仁者必有勇，勇
zhě bù bì yǒu rén
者不必有仁。"

The Master said, "One who has accumulated moral power will
certainly also possess eloquence; but he who has eloquence does
not necessarily possess moral power. A Good Man will certainly
also possess courage; but a brave man is not necessarily Good."

129

gǔ zhī xué zhě wèi jǐ jīn zhī xué zhě wèi rén

古 之 学 者 为 己, 今 之 学 者 为 人

zǐ yuē gǔ zhī xué zhě wèi jǐ jīn zhī xué zhě wèi rén

子曰: "古之学者为己, 今之学者为人。"

The Master said, "In old days, men studied for the sake of self-improvement; nowadays, men study in order to impress other people."

rén zhě bù yōu
仁者不忧

zǐ yuē　　　jūn zǐ dào zhě sān　　wǒ wú néng yān　　rén zhě bù yōu　　zhì zhě bù huò　　yǒng
子曰："君子道者三，我无能焉：仁者不忧，知者不惑，勇
zhě bù jù　　zǐ gòng yuē　　fū zǐ zì dào yě
者不惧。"子贡曰："夫子自道也。"

The Master said, "The Way of the true gentleman are three. I myself have met with success in none of them. For he that is really Good is never unhappy, he that is really wise is never perplexed, he that is really brave is never afraid." Tzu-kung said, "That, Master, is your own Way!"

知者不惑
zhì zhě bù huò

子曰："君子道者三，我无能焉：仁者不忧，知者不惑，勇
zǐ yuē   jūn zǐ dào zhě sān   wǒ wú néng yān   rén zhě bù yōu   zhì zhě bù huò   yǒng

者不惧。"子贡曰："夫子自道也。"
zhě bù jù   zǐ gòng yuē   fū zǐ zì dào yě

The Master said, "The Way of the true gentleman are three. I my
self have met with success in none of them. For he that is really
Good is never unhappy, he that is really wise is never perplexed, he
that is really brave is never afraid." Tzu-kung said, "That, Master, is
your own Way!"

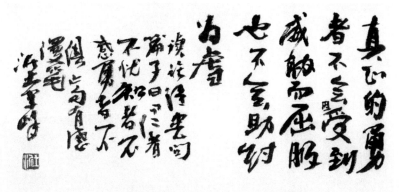

yǒng zhě bù jù
勇者不惧

zǐ yuē　　jūn zǐ dào zhě sān　　wǒ wú néng yān　　rén zhě bù yōu　　zhì zhě bù huò　　yǒng
子曰："君子道者三，我无能焉：仁者不忧，知者不惑，勇
zhě bù jù　　zǐ gòng yuē　　fū zǐ zì dào yě
者不惧。"子贡曰："夫子自道也。"

The Master said, "The Way of the true gentleman are three. I my
self have met with success in none of them. For he that is really
Good is never unhappy, he that is really wise is never perplexed, he
that is really brave is never afraid." Tzu-kung said, "That, Master, is
your own Way!"

133

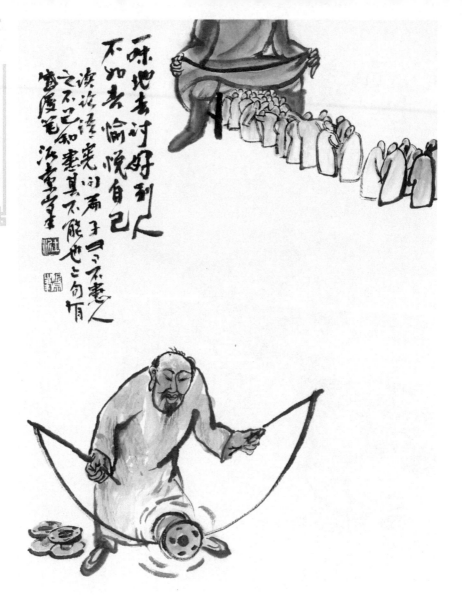

huàn qí bù néng

患其不能

zǐ yuē   bù huàn rén zhī bù jǐ zhī   huàn qí bù néng yě

子曰：“不患人之不己知，患其不能也。”

The Master said, "(A gentleman) does not grieve that people do not recognize his merits; he grieves at his own incapacities."

jì bù chēng qí lì   chēng qí dé yě
骥不称其力，称其德也

zǐ yuē   jì bù chēng qí lì   chēng qí dé yě
子曰："骥不称其力，称其德也。"

The Master said, "The horse Chi* was not famed for its strength but for its inner qualities."

---

* A famous horse of ancient times.

135

公平公正獎罰
分明是維護禮
會有序存在的
基本條件
淺飱語宽向而
子曰「何以報德以
直報怨以德
句有德沒笔
辛丑初秋江蘇峰畫

  yǐ zhí bào yuàn   yǐ dé bào dé

以 直 报 怨， 以 德 报 德

huò yuè   yǐ dé bào yuàn   hé rú   zǐ yuē   hé yǐ bào dé   yǐ zhí bào
或曰："以 德 报 怨，何 如？"子曰："何 以 报 德？以 直 报
yuàn   yǐ dé bào dé
怨，以 德 报 德。"

Someone said, "What about the saying 'Meet resentment with inner power?'" The Master said, "In that case, how is one to meet inner power? Rather, meet resentment with upright dealing and meet inner power with inner power."

xià xué ér shàng dá　　zhī wǒ zhě qí tiān hū
下学而上达，知我者其天乎

zǐ yuē　　　bù yuàn tiān　　bù yóu rén　　xià xué ér shàng dá　　zhī wǒ zhě qí tiān hū
子曰："不怨天，不尤人，下学而上达，知我者其天乎！"

The Master said, "I do not accuse Heaven, no do I lay the blame on men.* But the studies of men here below are felt on high, and perhaps after all I am known; not here, but in Heaven!"

---

* "A gentle man neither accuses Heaven nor blames men."

137

xián zhě bì shì
贤者辟世

zǐ yuē　　　xián zhě bì shì　　qí cì bì dì　　qí cì bì sè　　qí cì bì yán
子曰：“贤者辟世，其次辟地，其次辟色，其次辟言。”
zǐ yuē　　　zuò zhě qī rén yǐ
子曰：“作者七人矣。”

The Master said, "Best of all, to withdraw from one's generation;
next to withdraw to another land; next to leave because of a look;
next best to leave because of a word."* The Master said, "The makers
were seven …"

---

* If the Way does not prevail, it is better to flee altogether from the men of one's generation,
rather than to go round "perching first here, then there" as Confucius himself unsuccessfully
done, or to wait till the expression of the ruler's face betrays that he is meditating some
enormity; or worst of all, to wait till his words actually reveal his intention.

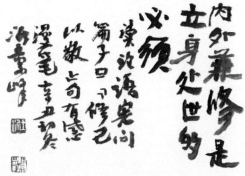

修己以敬
xiū jǐ yǐ jìng

子路问君子。子曰："修己以敬。"
zǐ lù wèn jūn zǐ   zǐ yuē   xiū jǐ yǐ jìng

Tzu-lu asked about the qualities of a true gentleman. The Master said, "He cultivates in himself the capacity to be diligent in his tasks."

Book XV

wèi líng gōng
卫灵公
(Duke Ling of Wei)

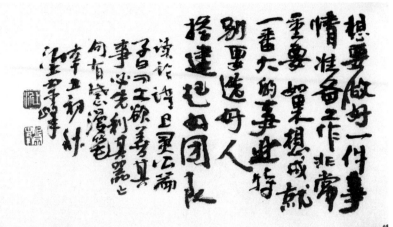

gōng yù shàn qí shì   bì xiān lì qí qì
工欲善其事，必先利其器

zǐ gòng wèn wéi rén   zǐ yuē   gōng yù shàn qí shì   bì xiān lì qí qì   jū shì bāng
子贡问为仁。子曰："工欲善其事，必先利其器。居是邦
yě   shì qí dà fū zhī xián zhě   yǒu qí shì zhī rén zhě
也，事其大夫之贤者，友其士之仁者。"

Tzu-kung asked how to become Good. The Master said, "A craftsman, if he means to do good work, must first sharpen his tools. In whatever State you dwell, take service with such of its officers as are worthy, make friends with such of knights as are Good."

rén wú yuǎn lǜ　　bì yǒu jìn yōu
人无远虑，必有近忧

zǐ yuē　　rén wú yuǎn lǜ　　bì yǒu jìn yōu
子曰："人无远虑，必有近忧。"

The Master said, "He who will not worry about what is far off will soon find something worse than worry close at hand."

gōng zì hòu ér bó zé yú rén
躬自厚而薄责于人

zǐ yuē　　gōng zì hòu ér bó zé yú rén　　zé yuǎn yuàn yǐ
子曰："躬自厚而薄责于人，则远怨矣。"

The Master said, "To demand much from oneself and little from others is the way (for a ruler) to banish discontent."

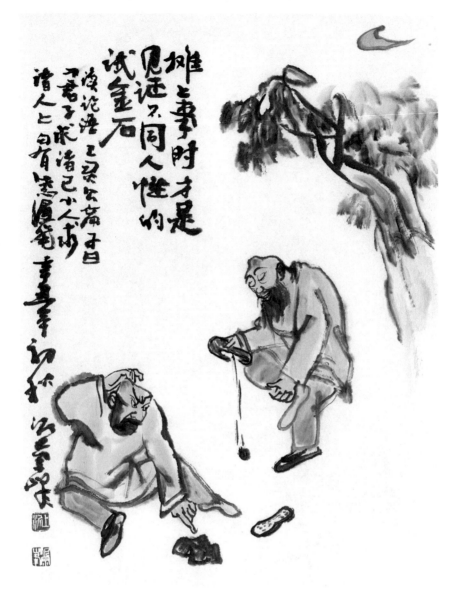

jūn zǐ qiú zhū jǐ   xiǎo rén qiú zhū rén

君子求诸己，小人求诸人

zǐ yuē   jūn zǐ qiú zhū jǐ   xiǎo rén qiú zhū rén

子曰："君子求诸己，小人求诸人。"

The Master said, "A gentleman is proud, but not quarrelsome, allies himself with individuals, but not with parties."

jūn zǐ bù yǐ yán jǔ rén bù yǐ rén fèi yán
君子不以言举人，不以人废言

zǐ yuē jūn zǐ bù yǐ yán jǔ rén bù yǐ rén fèi yán
子曰：“君子不以言举人，不以人废言。”

The Master said, "A gentleman does not accept men because of
what they say, nor reject sayings, because the speaker is what he is."

xiǎo bù rěn zé luàn dà móu
小不忍则乱大谋

zǐ yuē   qiǎo yán luàn dé   xiǎo bù rěn   zé luàn dà móu
子曰："巧言乱德。小不忍，则乱大谋。"

The Master said, "Clever talk can confound the workings of moral force, just as small impatiences can confound great project."

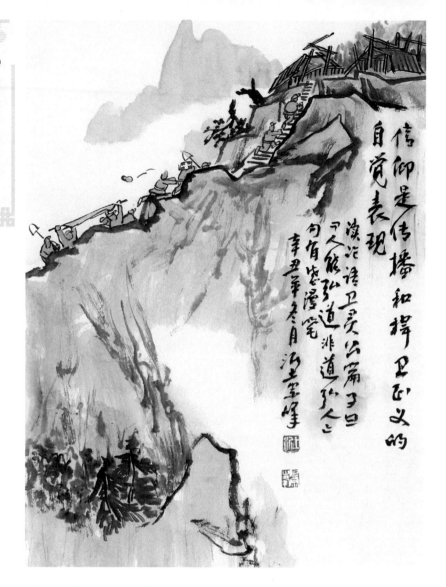

rén néng hóng dào   fēi dào hóng rén
人能弘道，非道弘人

zǐ yuē   rén néng hóng dào   fēi dào hóng rén
子曰：“人能弘道，非道弘人。”

The Master said, "A man can enlarge his Way; but there is no Way
that can enlarge a man."*

---

* Without effort on his part.

jūn zǐ móu dào bù móu shí
君子谋道不谋食

zǐ yuē jūn zǐ móu dào bù móu shí gēng yě něi zài qí zhōng yǐ xué yě lù zài
子曰："君子谋道不谋食。耕也，馁在其中矣；学也，禄在
qí zhōng yǐ jūn zǐ yōu dào bù yōu pín
其中矣。君子忧道不忧贫。"

The Master said, "A gentleman, in his plans, think of the Way; he does not think about how he is going to make a living. Even farming sometimes entails times of shortage; and even learning may incidentally lead to high pay. But a gentleman's anxieties concern the progress of the Way; he has no anxiety concerning poverty."

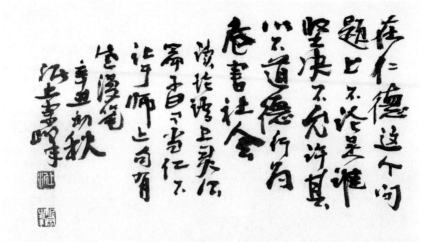

dāng rén bù ràng
当仁不让

zǐ yuē　　　dāng rén　　bù ràng yú shī
子曰："当仁，不让于师。"

The Master said, "When it comes to Goodness, one need not avoid competing with one's teacher."

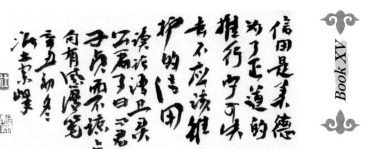

zhēn ér bù liàng
贞而不谅

zǐ yuē　　　 jūn zǐ zhēn ér bù liàng
子曰：“君子贞而不谅。”

The Master said, "From a gentleman consistency is expected, but not blind fidelity."

151

人的价值取向
不同欢·其无法
同心同德
读论语
正灵
仏篇曰子曰
"道不同不相为
谋"句有感而
漫笔·壬申初秋
深圳蝶

dào bù tóng bù xiāng wéi móu
道不同，不相为谋

zǐ yuē dào bù tóng bù xiāng wéi móu
子曰："道不同，不相为谋。"

The Master said, "With those who follow a different Way, it is useless to take counsel."

Book XVI

ji shi
季氏 (Chief of Ji Clan)

_{jì} _{lái} _{zhī} _{zé} _{ān} _{zhī}
既来之，则安之

_{kǒng zǐ yuē} _{fú rú shì} _{gù yuǎn rén bù fú} _{zé xiū wén dé yǐ lái zhī} _{jì lái}
孔子曰："夫如是，故远人不服，则修文德以来之。既来
_{zhī} _{zé} _{ān} _{zhī}
之，则安之。"

Master K'ung said, "If such a state of affairs exists, yet the people of far-off lands still do not submit, then the ruler must attract them by enhancing the prestige of his culture; and when they have been duly attracted, he contents them. And where there is contentment there will be no upheavals."

益者三友

yì zhě sān yǒu

kǒng zǐ yuē　　　yǒu zhí　　yǒu liàng　　yǒu duō wén　　yì yǐ

孔子曰："友直，友谅，友多闻，益矣。"

Master K'ung said, "Friendship with the upright, with the true-to-death, and with those who have heard much is profitable."

yì zhě sān lè
益者三乐

孔子曰：kǒng zǐ yuē "乐节礼乐，lè jié lǐ yuè 乐道人之善，lè dào rén zhī shàn 乐多贤友，lè duō xián yǒu 益矣。yì yǐ"

Master K'ung said, "The pleasure got from the due ordering of ritual and music, the pleasure got from discussing the good points in conduct of others, the pleasure of having many wise friends is profitable."

jūn zǐ yǒu sān jiè
君子有三戒

kǒng zǐ yuē   jūn zǐ yǒu sān jiè   shào zhī shí   xuè qì wèi dìng   jiè zhī zài sè   jí
孔子曰："君子有三戒：少之时，血气未定，戒之在色；及
qí zhuàng yě   xuè qì fāng gāng   jiè zhī zài dòu   jí qí lǎo yě   xuè qì jì shuāi   jiè
其壮也，血气方刚，戒之在斗；及其老也，血气既衰，戒
zhī zài dé
之在得。"

Master K'ung said, "There are three things against which a
gentleman is on his guard. In his youth, before his blood and vital
humours have settled down, he is on his guard against lust. Having
reached his prime, when the blood and vital humours have finally
hardened, he is on his guard against strife. Having reached old age,
when the blood and vital humours are already decaying, he is on his
guard against avarice."

jūn zǐ yǒu sān wèi
君子有三畏

kǒng zǐ yuē   jūn zǐ yǒu sān wèi   wèi tiān mìng   wèi dà rén   wèi shèng rén zhī yán
孔子曰："君子有三畏：畏天命，畏大人，畏圣人之言。
xiǎo rén bù zhī tiān mìng ér bù wèi yě   xiá dà rén   wǔ shèng rén zhī yán
小人不知天命而不畏也，狎大人，侮圣人之言。"

Master K'ung said, "There are three things that a gentleman fears:
he fears the will of Heaven, he fears great men, he fears the words of
the Divine Sages. The small man does not know the will of Heaven
and so does not fear it. He treats great men with contempt, and
scoffs at the words of the Divine Sages."

xué ér zhī zhī
学而知之

kǒng zǐ yuē　　shēng ér zhī zhī zhě shàng yě　　xué ér zhī zhī zhě cì yě　　kùn ér xué zhī
孔子曰："生而知之者上也，学而知之者次也；困而学之，
yòu qí cì yě　　kùn ér bù xué　　mín sī wéi xià yǐ
又其次也；困而不学，民斯为下矣。"

Master K'ung said, "Highest are those who are born wise. Next are those who become wise by learning. After them come those who have to toil painfully in order to acquire learning. Finally, to the lowest class of the common people belong those who toil painfully without ever managing to learn."

Book XVII

阳货 (Yang Huo,
Offical in the Ji Clan)

xìng xiāng jìn   xí xiāng yuǎn
性 相 近， 习 相 远

zǐ yuē   xìng xiāng jìn yè   xí xiāng yuǎn yè
子曰：“性相近也，习相远也。”

The Master said, "By nature, near together; by practice for apart."*

---

*   This proverbial saying has wide possibilities of application. It here presumably means
that goodness is a matter of training and application and not an inborn quality.

gōng zé bù wǔ　　kuān zé dé zhòng
恭则不侮，宽则得众

zǐ　yuē　　gōng　kuān　xìn　mǐn　huì　gōng zé bù wǔ　　kuān zé dé zhòng
（子）曰："恭、宽、信、敏、惠。恭则不侮，宽则得众，
xìn zé rén rèn yān　mǐn zé yǒu gōng　huì zé zú yǐ shǐ rén
信则人任焉，敏则有功，惠则足以使人。"

The Master said, "Courtesy, breadth, good faith, diligence, and clemency. 'He who is courteous is not scorned, he who is broad wins the multitude, he who is of good faith is trusted by the people, he who is diligent succeeds in all he undertakes, he who is clement can get service from the people.'"

163

道听途说

dào tīng tú shuō
道听途说

zǐ yuē   dào tīng ér tú shuō   dé zhī qì yě
子曰: "道听而涂说, 德之弃也。"

The Master said, "To tell in the lane what you have heard on the highroad is to throw merit away."

huàn dé huàn shī
患得患失

zǐ yuē   bǐ fū kě yǔ shì jūn yě yú zāi   qí wèi dé zhī yě   huàn dé zhī   jì dé
子曰："鄙夫可与事君也与哉？其未得之也，患得之。既得
zhī   huàn shī zhī   gǒu huàn shī zhī   wú suǒ bù zhì yǐ
之，患失之。苟患失之，无所不至矣。"

The Master said, "How could one ever possibly serve one's prince alongside of such low-down creatures? Before they have got office, they think about nothing but how to get it; and when they have got it, all they care about is to avoid losing it. And as soon as they see themselves in the slightest danger of losing it, there is no length to which they will not go."

Book XVIII

微子
(Wei Zi,
Founder of
the State of Song)

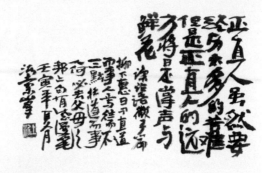

zhí dào ér shì rén
直道而事人

liú xià huì wéi shì shī　　sān chù　　rén yuē　　　　zǐ wèi kě yǐ qù hū　　　　yuē　　zhí
柳下惠为士师，三黜。人曰：“子未可以去乎？”曰：“直
dào ér shì rén　　yān wǎng ér bù sān chù　　wǎng dào ér shì rén　　hé bì qù fù mǔ zhī
道而事人，焉往而不三黜？枉道而事人，何必去父母之
bāng
邦？”

When Liu-hsia Hui was Leader of the Knights,* he was three times dismissed. People said to him, "Surely you would do well to seek service elsewhere?" He said, "If I continue to serve men in honest ways, where can I go and not be three times dismissed? If, on the other hand, I am willing to serve men by crooked ways, what need is there for me to leave the land of my father and mother?"

---

* A comparatively humble post. Its occupant was chiefly concerned with criminal cases.

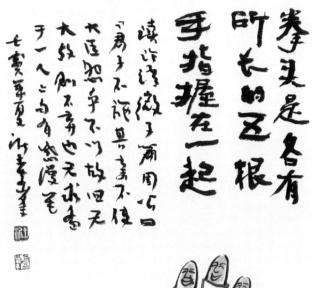

wú qiú bèi yú yì rén

无求备于一人

zhōu gōng wèi lǔ gōng yuē   jūn zǐ bù shī qí qīn   bù shǐ dà chén yuàn hū bù yǐ   gù jiù
周公谓鲁公曰："君子不施其亲，不使大臣怨乎不以。故旧
wú dà gù   zé bù qì yě   wú qiú bèi yú yì rén
无大故，则不弃也。无求备于一人。"

The Duke of Chou addressed the Duke of Lu,* saying: "A gentleman never discards his kinsmen; nor does he ever give occasion to his chief retainers to chafe at not being used. None who have been long in his service does he ever dismiss without grave cause. He does not except one man to be capable of everything."

_____
* His son.

Book XIX

子 张 (Zi Zhang,
Student of Confucius)

shì jiàn wēi zhì mìng

士见危致命

zǐ zhāng yuē　　　　shì jiàn wēi zhì mìng　　jiàn dé sī yì　　jì sī jìng　　sāng sī āi　　qí
子张曰："士见危致命，见得思义，祭思敬，丧思哀，其
kě yǐ yǐ
可已矣。"

Tzu-chang said, "A knight who confronted with danger is ready to
lay down his life, who confronted with the chance of gain thanks
first of right, who judges sacrifice by the degree of reverence shown
and mourning by the degree of grief—such a one is all that can be
desired."

_{zūn} _{xián} _{róng} _{zhòng}

尊贤容众

_{zǐ zhāng yuē}　　　_{yì hū wú suǒ wén}　　_{jūn zǐ zūn xián ér róng zhòng}　_{jiā shàn ér guān bù néng}
子张曰:"异乎吾所闻:君子尊贤而容众,嘉善而矜不能。"

Tzu-chang said, "That is different from what I have been told: A gentleman reverences those that excel, but 'finds room* for all'; He commends the food and pities the incapable."

---

* Tolerates.

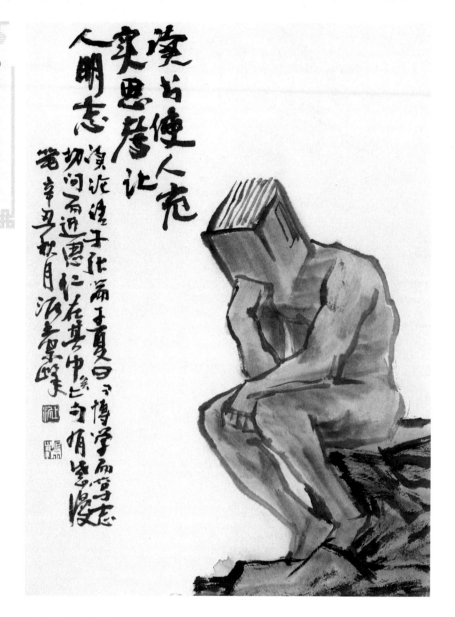

bó xué dǔ zhì
博学笃志

zǐ xià yuē   bó xué ér dǔ zhì   qiè wèn ér jìn sī   rén zài qí zhōng yǐ
子夏曰: "博学而笃志, 切问而近思, 仁在其中矣。"

Tzu-hsia said, "One who studies widely and with set purpose, who
questions earnestly, then thinks for himself about what he was
heard—such a one will incidentally achieve Goodness."

jūn zǐ yǒu sān biàn
君子有三变

zǐ xià yuē　　　jūn zǐ yǒu sān biàn　wàng zhī yǎn rán　　jí zhī yě wēn　tīng qí yán yě lì
子夏曰:"君子有三变:望之俨然, 即之也温, 听其言也厉。"

Tzu-hsia said, "A gentleman has three varying aspects: seen from afar, he looks sever; when approached, he is found to be mild; when heard speaking, he turns out to be incisive."

左非原则的事情和问题上吴活变通才是聪者的人生

濒临涣子张篇

子夏曰「大德不通闲小德出入可也」自有感漫笔

壬午暮春

dà dé bù yú xián
大德不逾闲

zǐ xià yuē   dà dé bù yú xián   xiǎo dé chū rù kě yě
子夏曰: "大德不逾闲, 小德出入可也。"

Tzu-hsia said, "So long as in undertakings of great moral import a man does not 'cross the barrier,' in undertakings of little moral import he may 'come out and go in.'"*

---

* In matters such as loyalty, keeping promises, obedience to parents, the laws which govern his conduct are absolute. In lesser matters he is allowed a certain latitude.

yǒu shǐ yǒu zhōng
有始有终

zǐ xià wén zhī yuē jūn zǐ zhī dào yān kě wū yě yǒu shǐ yǒu zú zhě
子夏闻之，曰：" …… 君子之道，焉可诬也？有始有卒者，
qí wéi shèng rén hū
其惟圣人乎！"

Tzu-hsia, hearing of this, said, "... In the Way of Gentleman, there can be no bluff. It is only the Divine Sage who embraces in himself both the first step and the last."

shì ér yōu zé xué　　xué ér yōu zé shì
仕而优则学，学而优则仕

zǐ xià yuē　　shì ér yōu zé xué·　xué ér yōu zé shì
子夏曰：“仕而优则学，学而优则仕。”

Tzu-hsia said, "The energy that a man has left over after doing his duty to the State, he should devote to study; the energy that he has left after studying, he should devote to service of the State."

jūn zǐ zhī guò
君子之过

zǐ gòng yuē   jūn zǐ zhī guò yě   rú rì yuè zhī shí yān   guò yě   rén jiē jiàn zhī
子贡曰："君子之过也，如日月之食焉。过也，人皆见之；
gēng yě   rén jiē yǎng zhī
更也，人皆仰之。"

Tzu-kung said, "The faults of a gentleman are like eclipses of the sun or moon. If he does wrong, everyone sees it. When he corrects his fault, every gaze is turned up towards him."

Book XX

yáo yuē
尧曰 (Yao Spoke)

huì ér bù fèi

惠而不费

zǐ yuē   jūn zǐ huì ér bù fèi   láo ér bù yuàn   yù ér bù tān   tài ér bù jiāo
子曰："君子惠而不费，劳而不怨，欲而不贪，泰而不骄，
wēi ér bù měng
威而不猛。"

The Master said, "A gentle man can be bounteous without extravagance, can get work out of people without arousing resentment, has longings but is never covetous, is proud but never insolent, inspires awe but is never ferocious."

láo ér bù yuàn
劳而不怨

zǐ yuē　　jūn zǐ huì ér bù fèi　　láo ér bù yuàn　　yù ér bù tān　　tài ér bù jiāo
子曰："君子惠而不费，劳而不怨，欲而不贪，泰而不骄，
wēi ér bù měng
威而不猛。"

The Master said, "A gentle man can be bounteous without extravagance, can get work out of people without arousing resentment, has longings but is never covetous, is proud but never insolent, inspires awe but is never ferocious."

yù ér bù tān

欲而不贪

zǐ yuē　　jūn zǐ huì ér bù fèi　　láo ér bù yuàn　　yù ér bù tān　　tài ér bù jiāo
子曰：“君子惠而不费，劳而不怨，<u>欲而不贪</u>，泰而不骄，
wēi ér bù měng
威而不猛。”

The Master said, "A gentle man can be bounteous without extravagance, can get work out of people without arousing resentment, <u>has longings but is never covetous</u>, is proud but never insolent, inspires awe but is never ferocious."

<ruby>泰 tài</ruby> <ruby>而 ér</ruby> <ruby>不 bù</ruby> <ruby>骄 jiāo</ruby>

泰而不骄

子曰：“君子惠而不费，劳而不怨，欲而不贪，泰而不骄，
威而不猛。”

The Master said, "A gentle man can be bounteous without extravagance, can get work out of people without arousing resentment, has longings but is never covetous, is proud but never insolent, inspires awe but is never ferocious."

wēi ér bù měng
威而不猛

zǐ yuē　　 jūn zǐ huì ér bù fèi　　 láo ér bù yuàn　　 yù ér bù tān　　 tài ér bù jiāo
子曰：“君子惠而不费，劳而不怨，欲而不贪，泰而不骄，
wēi ér bù měng
威而不猛。”

The Master said, "A gentle man can be bounteous without extravagance, can get work out of people without arousing resentment, has longings but is never covetous, is proud but never insolent, inspires awe but is never ferocious."

jūn zǐ zhī mìng

君子知命

kǒng zǐ yuē 孔子曰：" bù zhī mìng 不知命， wú yǐ wéi jūn zǐ yě 无以为君子也； bù zhī lǐ 不知礼， wú yǐ lì yě 无以立也；不 bù
zhī yán 知言， wú yǐ zhī rén yě 无以知人也。"

The Master said, "He who does not understand the will of Heaven cannot be regarded as a gentleman. He who does not know the rites cannot take his stand. He who does not understand words cannot understand people."

不知礼，无以立也

孔子曰：“不知命，无以为君子也；不知礼，无以立也；不知言，无以知人也。”

The Master said, "He who does not understand the will of Heaven cannot be regarded as a gentleman. He who does not know the rites cannot take his stand. He who does not understand words cannot understand people."

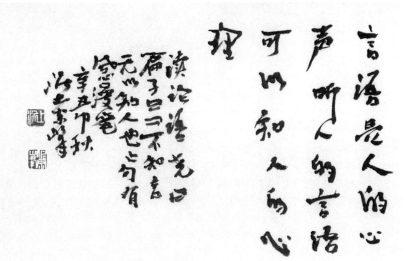

言语是人的心
声听人的言语
可以知人的心

演论语光曰
扁子曰言不知言
无以知人也之句有
感漫笔
辛丑仲秋
必之素峰

bù zhī yán　　wú yǐ zhī rén yě
不知言，无以知人也

kǒng zǐ yuē　　　bù zhī mìng　　wú yǐ wéi jūn zǐ yě　　bù zhī lǐ　　wú yǐ lì yě　　bù
孔子曰："不知命，无以为君子也；不知礼，无以立也；不
zhī yán　　wú yǐ zhī rén yě
知言，无以知人也。"

The Master said, "He who does not understand the will of Heaven cannot be regarded as a gentleman. He who does not know the rites cannot take his stand. <u>He who does not understand words cannot understand people.</u>"

189

POSTSCRIPT

The Illustrated Analects: Selected Teachings is a project I completed over the past eight years during my spare time outside of work. If one's hobbies can become their profession, it should be considered a fortunate occurrence. However, when hobbies cannot transition into a profession and become expertise, let's leave expertise for life and leave the profession for labor.

Confucius's words, "志于道，据于德，依于仁，游于艺" (Set your heart upon the Way, support yourself by its power, learn upon Goodness, seek distraction in the arts), serve as my standard for seeking art. The pursuit of art is an exploratory process. Using ink-wash comics to portray China's excellent traditional culture is a beneficial attempt and the main theme of this book. I selected over 100 sentences from the twenty chapters of *The Analects* and presented them in comic language. This allows the work to cover the main ideas of *The Analects* while striving to be interesting, emotional, intriguing, and insightful. It enables viewers to understand the visual functionality while enjoying the art. The function of painting, in simple terms, is to make people feel beautiful, fun, dynamic, insightful, and thought-provoking after seeing it. The painting should be distinctive, with varied techniques, and the scenes should not be too similar; one should seek individuality between adherence to tradition and the pursuit of innovation.

In the hearts of a hundred readers, there are a hundred Confuciuses. Similar viewpoints differ only in perspective. Interpreting *The Analects* under the premise of respecting Confucianism and accommodating talents, those who can speak logically and form their own opinions are all worthy of respect. This is different from subjects like mathematics, physics, and chemistry, where there must be a standard answer.

I humbly request your guidance on any inappropriate aspects of the compilation and illustration.

"过, 则勿惮改" (If you have made a mistake, do not be afraid of admitting the fact and amending your ways).

Ni Zongfeng

August 2023

ABOUT THE ILLUSTRATOR

NI ZONGFENG, Vice Chairman of the Shandong Cartoonist Association and a member of the China Artists Association, currently serves as the Secretary-General of The International Chamber of Commerce for Culture Industry of Shandong Province. Born in Jinan, Ni has been awarded the Silver Prize for Chinese News Art and has participated in international comic exhibitions in Japan, Belgium, and South Korea. He was honored with a special award from the Yomiuri International Manga Competition judging committee in Japan.